AL
TICE
dbook

Understanding RIGHT AND WRONG

Michael Rosen and Annemarie Young

rosen publishing's
rosen
central

This edition published in 2020 by:
The Rosen Publishing Group, Inc.
29 East 21st Street
New York, NY 10010

First Edition

Cataloging-in-Publication Data

Names: Rosen, Michael. | Young, Annemarie.
Title: Understanding right and wrong / Michael Rosen and Annemarie Young.
Description: New York : Rosen Central, 2020. | Series: Social justice handbook | Includes glossary and index.
Identifiers: ISBN 9781725346864 (pbk.) | ISBN 9781725346871 (library bound)
Subjects: LCSH: Ethics—Juvenile literature | Right and wrong—Juvenile literature. | Values—Juvenile literature. | Decision making—Moral and ethical aspects—Juvenile literature. Right and wrong—Juvenile literature.
Classification: LCC BJ1012.R67 2019 | DDC 170—dc23

Manufactured in the United States of America

Copyright © 2020 Wayland, a division of Hachette Children's Group

Editor: Nicola Edwards
Designer: Rocket Design [East Anglia] Ltd
Artwork by Oli Frape

Picture acknowledgements:
Cover photo: Ariel Skelley / iStock / Getty Images Plus. Cover design element: CS Stock / Shutterstock; p5 (clockwise from top left): © Claude Schneider; © Walter White; © Jon Armstrong; Richard Rieser; br Wikimedia Commons; p6 Courtesy of Goldsmiths, University of London; p7 Wikimedia Commons; p8t Anthony Robinson, b Wikimedia Commons; p13 Wikimedia Commons; p14 and p15t (backgrounds) Shutterstock.com; p14 Shutterstock.com; p15 (both) Wikimedia Commons; p17 Wikimedia Commons; p19 Adam Kliczek/Wikimedia Commons; p21 Sergey Kohl / Shutterstock .com; p22 Richard Rieser; p24 nikolpetr / Shutterstock.com; p25 Shutterstock.com; p27 Igor Grochev / Shutterstock.com; p28 © Jon Armstrong; p29 A. Ricardo / Shutterstock.com; p30 Shutterstock .com; p32 © Claude Schneider; p33 Michael Candelori / Shutterstock.com; p34 Shutterstock.com; p35 Shutterstock.com; p37 Wikimedia Commons; p39 Wikimedia Commons; p40 © Walter White; p43 Wikimedia Commons; p45 Shutterstock.com.

Contents

What Is This Book About?

Every day we make decisions that are underpinned by our ideas of what is right and wrong. But where do these ideas come from? Where do our values come from and who decides which values are used in a society? This book is not going to tell you what to think. Our aim is to get you to think for yourselves about these and many other related questions.

We think it's important that everyone should think about life's big questions, and never just accept what they are told. This doesn't mean that you can't continue to hold the ideas or values that you had, but if you do, you'll know that those values are your own and not just an unthinking acceptance of someone else's ideas.

How does the book work?

We've chosen topics that are strongly connected to the values people hold and to their ideas of what is right and wrong, such as democracy, justice, fairness, prejudice and discrimination, education, climate change, and war. We'll give you information about each topic and ask questions related to them to get you thinking about your own values.

Of course, we couldn't possibly fit into this one book all the information you need in order to answer all the questions. Instead, we'll provide you with information about some key principles and institutions – such as the rule of law, and the key principles of democracy – and other aspects of the questions, such as information on wars or climate change.

⬇ How can the problems of pollution and climate change be solved? When air pollution in cities is often too bad for children to play outside, should governments ban the combustion engine and phase in electric cars?

We'll also ask you to find out more about some of the issues and how they relate to your life and your values. For example, if your country went to war, would you take part? If your country was invaded, would you resist?

The people in the book

We'll tell you about ourselves, and how we developed our own ideas and values. You will also hear from four people – Laura Bates, Richard Rieser, Tulip Siddiq, and Alex Wheatle – who'll discuss their own experiences and thoughts about right and wrong. In addition, there are quotes from other people spread through the book.

Laura Bates

Alex Wheatle

Richard Rieser

Tulip Siddiq

> "To be neutral in a situation of injustice is to have chosen sides already. It is to support the status quo."
>
> Archbishop Desmond Tutu

At the end

On the last two pages, we'll ask you to reflect on what you've read, and on the discussions you've had while reading the book. We'll ask:

- Did you change your mind about anything?

- What principles and values do you think can best convey your ideas about right and wrong?

- What can we do to bring about what we believe is right?

My Experience

Michael Rosen was born in 1946. He's a writer for adults and children, a broadcaster, and Professor of Children's Literature at Goldsmiths, University of London.

☀ Ideals

Every one of us has an idea of what the words "right" and "wrong" mean. The ideas about "right" are sometimes called "ideals." This means they are ideas about the best ways to behave, although we may not always be able to live up to them.

We may not be able to write down all our ideas about right and wrong, but we have another way of expressing right and wrong – through our actions. Sometimes what we say is right or wrong and what we actually do are different. People call this "hypocritical" which is itself often described as "wrong."

For example, when I was at school, I would have said that bullying is wrong and yet sometimes I teased people in a bullying sort of a way. Then I changed schools, someone teased me, and I hated it. This showed me I had been hypocritical. It showed me that something I had done was wrong and I tried to change. If I heard myself being like that I tried to check myself but it hasn't always worked. This tells me several things about right and wrong: it's a complicated mix of "ideals" and actions; we can learn from experience; it's not easy to live up to ideals, but for the sake of equality and fairness, it's better to try than not try.

☀ Where do ideas about right and wrong come from?

As you're reading this, you could ask yourself, "Where do I get my ideas about right and wrong from?"

When I ask myself this, I can see that to start off with, the biggest influence on my life was my parents. When they were children, they were very poor but they studied hard and both of them became teachers. They rejected the religion of their grandparents and tried to work out their own "universal" principles: things like, all people should be equal, people shouldn't exploit each other or discriminate against each other, and people have the right to build this equal world. That was the "ideal." The big problem for them was that in

⬆ In the 1960s in Selma, Alabama, people marched in support of equal voting rights for black people in the USA.

countries where some leaders said they were building this new "right" society, they were exploiting and discriminating all over again!

☀ As I was growing up

As I was growing up, they told me about all this.

In 1960 I was 14, so the 1960s covered my late teens and early twenties. It was just when the world was in ferment about civil rights, feminism, war, work, poverty, inequality, domination of one set of countries over other countries.

At school and university, I loved having conversations about all this. We talked about the rights and wrongs of education, work, society, and war. I went to meetings and conferences and took part in demonstrations. I went to see plays, listened to music (songs,

mostly) that talked of these things, and I studied writers and thinkers.

I argued with my parents about some of this. Sometimes I influenced them, sometimes they influenced me. I was very lucky: even though we argued, they loved me and I loved them. And here I am, helping to write a book about right and wrong, inviting you to think and talk about it! I like to think they would think that was "right." This tells me that love has a lot to do with right and wrong, too.

THiNK about

Talk to your parents or other people at home about their ideas of right and wrong. What are they and where did your parents get them from?

"... love has a lot to do with right and wrong."

My Experience

Annemarie Young

Annemarie Young was born in 1950. She was a publisher, and she now writes stories and information books for children and young people.

※ My parents' influence

My earliest ideas about right and wrong came from my parents, particularly from my mother, who was very clear about her notions of justice and fairness and right or wrong, especially in our treatment of others. My father shared her fundamental values, but they sometimes disagreed on details, and when they did, their discussions were always interesting!

My parents' values were reinforced by the nuns at school. Many of those ideals were positive and sensible: being kind to others, especially those less fortunate, doing no harm (the Golden Rule, see page 12).

But as I got older I found that other ideas and practices – for example ones that implied women were secondary to men – contradicted what I believed to be right. I began to question other Catholic teachings and finally realized that I was a humanist and didn't believe in religion.

Another influence was being the child of immigrant parents. I grew up feeling very much an outsider, and this made me empathize with those treated as the "other."

※ Witnessing injustice

On a trip from Australia to Europe in 1970, my parents were shocked by the day-to-day manifestations of apartheid in Durban in South Africa, where the ship briefly docked. They were appalled at the "Whites Only" benches and the inferior facilities reserved for "Blacks."

⬆ This was one of the signs used in apartheid-era South Africa.

However, my father couldn't believe that his beloved adopted country, Australia, could also be racist. I had to convince him that parts of the White Australia policy (see panel) still existed. He also found my descriptions of government policies on Aboriginal people hard to believe because they were so blatantly unjust.

☀ Campaigning for justice

My sense of fairness and justice developed into a belief that I should actively campaign for justice. I started by supporting groups against apartheid in South Africa and those seeking justice for Aboriginal people in Australia. Then I joined the campaign against the Vietnam War, particularly Australia's role in it.

My values continued to develop as I grew older. Many experiences reinforced my notions of justice. Once, while I was living in China in 1983, an open truck drove past full of men with crosses marked on the backs of their shaved heads. I was told they were being taken for public execution. I still shudder at the image. I believe the death penalty is always wrong, that it is state-sanctioned murder. Worst of all, what if an executed person turns out to be innocent?

The White Australia policy

Australia's long-term immigration policies effectively barred people of non-European descent from entering the country. Things slowly changed from 1949 until the Racial Discrimination Act of 1975 made racially-based selection unlawful.

The Stolen Generations

Between 1910-1970, the government forcibly removed many Aboriginal children from their families "for their own good"– these children are known as the Stolen Generations. This racist and inhumane policy was based on the assumption of the superiority of white culture.

☀ Putting values into practice

I now write books with my husband, Anthony Robinson, to give a voice to children who are usually not heard. We have written books in which refugee children, street children, and young Palestinians living under occupation in the West Bank, tell their stories.

I don't always live up to my own ideals, but I try! For me, the most important issue is identifying unfairness and injustice and determining what I can do to combat them, while recognizing that we cannot do everything for everyone.

"My values continued to develop as I grew older."

What Do We Mean by Right and Wrong?

Principles – what we think is "right"

When we use the word "right" in this book, we are talking about what are called principles or ideals. These are the rules and conventions we develop to help us run our lives. When we think these rules and conventions have been broken, we say this is wrong.

This makes it sound very simple. It's not. Consider this, for example: if I was a political leader, I might say that it's "right" that in my country – Happyland – we need to get rid of all left-handed people. If enough people agreed with me, I could become the President and pass a law to stop left-handed people getting certain jobs. Left-handed people might say that this was unfair and protest. I might then say they were dangerous and jail or exile them. All the time I would be saying that what I was doing was "right."

The idea of discriminating against left-handed people might not seem very reasonable to us now, but it could work like this: a group of people with a set of beliefs, including that left-handedness is "evil," gain enough supporters to elect the leader of the country, and that leader can then make laws based on those beliefs.

Are there any principles that are right or wrong whatever the circumstances?

It's clear from the fictional example that we can't easily say it's absolutely the case that something is right or wrong. It's obvious that not everyone in Happyland would agree with a law to stop left-handed people from getting good jobs. Many people, and not just those who are left-handed, would think it was quite unfair. The idea of fairness is very important in determining the principles we live by. We'll look at fairness in more detail later.

As you can see, people don't always agree on what is right and wrong, fair or unfair, and therefore on how we should organize and run our lives.

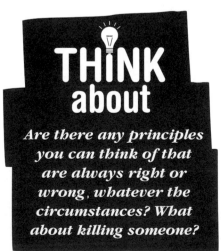

THiNK about

Are there any principles you can think of that are always right or wrong, whatever the circumstances? What about killing someone?

Principles – personal and social

Ideas about right and wrong are learned through a mix of social interaction – how we interact with other people – and what we hear, read, and see around us.

It's important to remember that these ideas aren't just personal, like say, whether it's right to boast about yourself. They are also social, like how we build and maintain relationships, families, communities, society and, ultimately, the whole world.

So, taking that in order, questions of right and wrong can be about, for example, whether both people in a relationship have an equal voice, whether the males and females in a family unit do equal amounts of work, what's right and wrong for our street, schools, hospitals, villages, towns, cities, and the environment, and what's best for the country we live in and the world. In effect, it is about what is best for the greatest number of people, not just for the individual.

However, none of this is simple or straightforward!

"The greatest happiness of the greatest number" was an idea first put forward by the philosopher and legal and social reformer Jeremy Bentham (1748–1832). This became the foundation of many of our morals and legislation.

THiNK about

Should or could all harmful drugs, including nicotine and alcohol, be banned or regulated?

What might seem to be right for me as an individual might not be right for my neighbor, or what's right for my town might not be right for the people living in the next town. What seems to be right for my country might not be right for the world. We have to work these things out using systems of "governance" such as councils, parliaments, and international forums like the United Nations.

Government or the individual?

Governments already ban or regulate certain things that are harmful – for example, weapons, certain drugs, and driving speeds. Some drugs, like cocaine, are illegal, but that doesn't stop some people from using them. Similarly, knowing that long-term misuse of some legal drugs, such as nicotine (cigarettes) and alcohol, is harmful doesn't stop some people misusing them, even though this often causes serious physical and mental health issues.

Do you think that it's up to the individual to decide if it's right or wrong to take drugs? You might like to consider the fact that illegal drugs are trafficked, distributed, and sold by criminals, and that excessive drug taking and drinking of alcohol affects society and those closest to the user.

11

Where Do Values Come From?

For thousands of years, all over the world, the main way people learned about right and wrong was through the sacred texts of their religions, including (in alphabetical order), Buddhism, Christianity, Hinduism, Islam, Judaism, and books written by religious thinkers and leaders. At the same time – and now more so than ever – people have developed ideas about right and wrong with very little or no reference to a god or sacred texts, believing that morality comes out of human experience and personal honesty and responsibility.

The people who've written about these ideas might be philosophers, politicians, thinkers, writers, and teachers, such as Confucius, Mary Wollstonecraft, Karl Marx, Maya Angelou, and thousands of others.

However, there is one basic principle that underlies humanism and also seems to be universal to all traditions – religious and philosophical. This is known as the Golden Rule:

> ## "Treat other people in the way you would like to be treated yourself."
> ### The Golden Rule

One among many

How does the Golden Rule work? Here's a way of thinking about it: you are an individual and yet you are always in a relationship with other people who influence what you think about right and wrong – at home, at school, around your local neighborhood and when you travel away from home. You read news reports and hear about wars, disasters, famines, diseases, great achievements, and much more, and this too has an influence on your ideas about right and wrong.

One way to help ourselves sort this difficult matter out is to look around at the world and at history.

Values are not fixed

Once we do this, the first thing we notice is that ideas about what is right and wrong are not "fixed." For example, if you go back to 1800 in Britain and America, you would find that many white people thought that slavery was right because white people, they would have said, were superior to black people. When you read what people said and did in the past or you look around the world, you can find examples of people saying that:

- men are superior to women,
- gay people should be put in prison,
- murderers should be executed in public.

Such ideas become more than just ideas when they are made into laws. Laws are the way in which a society or country puts into practice what a government has decided is right or wrong. This is called the "justice system" and you can see the police, the law courts, prisons, and the government all involved in this. Again, we have to remember that though at any given moment this system is all in place and settled, over time it changes and it varies from country to country.

THiNK about

Is it better to wait for those in power to change their minds? Or should we take action to change opinions and policy?

"Men make the moral code and they expect women to accept it."

Emmeline Pankhurst

➡ Emmeline Pankhurst, founder of the Women's Social and Political Union, was arrested several times during her fight to win the right for British women to vote.

How are values changed?

This reminds us that, in our world, these matters are set up by people expressing themselves through politics. Over time this has happened as a result of elections, demonstrations, rebellions, revolutions, and wars. For example, go back to 1800 in the United States and very few people were allowed to vote. That was thought by those in power to be right. It took the actions and changing opinions of many people to alter that situation. Many people were put in prison trying to win votes for all adults.

What Is Society?

Is it like a machine?

We all live in a "society." This doesn't simply mean that we live in a country or nation. Some people say that "society" is like a machine, where the parts are meshed together, each part having an effect on another one. If society was a car, you could see how turning the steering wheel makes the front wheels move. So for instance, in a society, farmers rear cattle which produce milk, which is bought by shops and supermarkets, where we then buy the milk. Over time, this becomes the "right" way to do things.

This way of describing society suggests it all works in "harmony," like a choir singing in tune together.

Or is society more complex and intertwined?

Another way of describing society says that, yes, we are all meshed together but the result is not fair. And this is not "right." You may hear on the news that the "economy is doing well" and yet millions of people might say at the same time that they are poorer, that the economy is not doing well for them, and that this is not "right." This suggests that the idea of society as a machine doesn't paint the whole picture. The car might be going forward but it's left some of the passengers behind!

Then again, people say that when the "economy is doing well" some people are indeed doing very well. How come? Is it because they work harder, or they are cleverer, or what? And is this right?

Maybe, say some, it's not so much that the passengers are left behind, rather that they are pushing the car along so that one or two people can sit in the car! If that describes the situation, would that be right?

How do societies change?

Let's stay with cars for the time being. Over time, they have changed and many more people have them. Some people think this is good and right. They say it's "progress." Others say that all these cars have ended up causing accidents, deaths and pollution: not so right.

There are two views of how society changes. One view is that we are generally getting better and better at getting things right for more and more people: we live longer, we are better at airing our views, there is less discrimination, even the poorest are better off than the poorest of a hundred years ago, we are wiping out diseases, more people are better educated than ever before. This suggests that society

is like a line on a graph going up, getting better and better.

Another view is that while some things are better, other things get worse. In other words, some things (like advances in medicine, the invention of labor-saving devices and votes for all) are right and some things, like wars, terrorism, inequality, pollution, famine, and climate change are wrong. Perhaps the graph looks more like a spiral going forwards and up and curving back down!

⬆ The spiral society: while technological advances in transportation have connected people and places like never before, roads have become increasingly congested and dangerous and the air more polluted.

Where are we now on the line or spiral?

Are we on the line going up or are we in a spiral? If it's the line, then we don't have to do anything different from what we're doing now. If it's the spiral then we have to come up with ideas for how to stop that "curving back down" effect. This is exactly where our different ideas about right and wrong come in.

THiNK about

What do you think? Is society more like a line, always making progress, or more like a spiral that goes up and down at different times?

What Is Democracy?

There are some forms of government where power is held by one person, as in dictatorships, or by a small number of individuals, like army generals or tribal leaders — and where the people have no real say in how the government works, or in replacing the government with another.

In contrast, democracy is based on the belief in freedom and equality between people. It describes a system of government in which power is usually held by representatives who are elected by a majority of those eligible to vote. There are almost as many different ways of organizing this system as there are democratic countries.

What happens when people disagree with laws?

Democratic societies allow people to protest and argue against laws they disagree with. As we've seen, ideas of what is fair and just change and it's often the case that changes in laws come about through protest as well as debate (see page 13).

Democracy requires compromise - groups with different interests and opinions must be willing to negotiate with each other.

In a democracy, one group does not always win everything it wants. Different combinations of groups win on different issues. But if one group is always excluded and fails to be heard, it may turn against democracy in anger and frustration, leading to civil unrest.

Key principles of a democracy

※ A political system for choosing and replacing a government through regular elections that are free and fair.

※ A government is chosen by a majority of the people, but the rights of those who voted for the opposition are respected, and the rights of minorities are protected in various ways.

※ The active participation of the people in what is called "civic life."

※ The protection of the human rights of all citizens, including freedom of expression.

※ Freedom of the press and media, without interference from the state.

※ The "rule of law" (see page 18), which applies equally to all citizens.

※ There are limits to what the government can do, based on a constitution, (not necessarily written) or other charter that sets out basic principles.

※ There are a number of different groups or parties, with different views, and there isn't one elite or group of elites that effectively have the power.

※ It is based on the values of tolerance, pragmatism, cooperation, and compromise.

Can democratically elected leaders become dictators?

Here is a well-known example of how a democratically elected government, through a series of clever moves, was able to end democracy, with far-reaching consequences.

In 1928, Adolf Hitler was the leader of the tiny Nazi Party in Germany, with only 12 seats in parliament. Then, in 1933, he was elected Chancellor of Germany with 230 seats. And from Chancellor he became a dictator within a matter of months.

Hitler used the excuse of a fire in the parliament building (the Reichstag) to pass the Reichstag Fire Decree, which suspended most civil liberties in Germany. He whipped up fear by insisting that the fire was the start of a Communist plot to take over Germany. Then a few months later he was able to pass a law called the Enabling Act. The Act was a special law that gave the Chancellor the power to pass laws by decree, without the involvement of the parliament. He was able to get the law passed in parliament by preventing – through arrests and intimidation – a large enough number of members of parliament from voting. In this way Hitler effectively abolished democracy and established himself as a dictator.

THiNK about

Find out why the Nazi Party became popular in Germany in the late 1920s and early 1930s, and how they came to power. Could something like this happen now, in this or another country?

⬆ Adolf Hitler gives the Nazi salute to a group of marching soldiers.

What Is Justice?

A simple definition of justice is that it is the quality of being fair and reasonable. And fairness means treating everyone equally or in a way that is right or reasonable (although, as we have seen, not everyone agrees on what reasonable means). What we are looking at here is justice as it is formalized in the laws of a country.

One of the most important features of modern democratic societies is the rule of law, which protects the rights of all citizens and limits the power of institutions, business, and even the power of government. Each country has its own justice system and they all work in different ways to implement the rule of law. For example, the justice systems in France, Germany, Italy, and the UK, among many others, are very different from the one in the United States.

Why do we send people to prison?

What is the main purpose of sending law-breakers to prison? Is it to rehabilitate them – help them get back to normal life after they've served their time – or simply to punish them? Those who believe that prisons should rehabilitate people say that it will make society safer. Those who focus on punishment are more concerned that the person "repay a debt to society."

The rule of law

This is a system of rules developed and agreed over time by the governing body in a country – such as Parliament in the UK or Congress in the US – which apply to all citizens. The rule of law places limits on the power of government, institutions and business and if anyone goes beyond these limits they are penalized or punished.

The main elements of the rule of law in liberal democracies are:

* All citizens are equal under the law. No one may be discriminated against on the basis of their race, religion, ethnic group, or gender.
* No one may be arbitrarily – randomly – arrested, imprisoned, or exiled.
* Torture and cruel and inhumane treatment are forbidden.
* If a person is detained, they have the right to know the charges against them, and to be presumed innocent until proven guilty according to the law.
* Anyone charged with a crime has the right to a fair and public trial by an impartial (unbiased) court (with competent, ethical, and independent representatives).
* No ruler, minister, political party, or other group can influence a judge's decision. Those in office cannot use their power to enrich themselves.
* No one may be taxed or prosecuted except by a law established in advance.
* No one is above the law, whatever their position in society.
* The law is fairly, impartially, and consistently enforced by courts that are independent of the other branches of government and other groups.

⬇ Pictured is a cell from Alcatraz, a high-security prison on Alcatraz Island, California. It was operational between 1934 and 1963, and the emphasis was on punishment rather than rehabilitation. It is now a museum.

"The prison system needs to be beneficial for the prisoners for the sake of their victims. If you are in there [prison] fighting for your life, you are not going to be able to get the new skills needed to make you more likely to succeed as a law-abiding citizen."

Erwin James, editor of a newspaper for people in prison. While himself in prison for murder, he was helped by a prison psychologist to "feel human," and to "understand the importance of moral values."

What happens when the law gets it wrong?

Miscarriages of justice happen when mistakes, deliberate or otherwise, are made in the process of charging and taking someone through the criminal justice system. The mistakes can be made by the police, lawyers, witnesses, judges, or juries; sometimes people make up evidence or simply lie. So, innocent people are sometimes convicted of crimes. These miscarriages of justice can take many years to put right, and some may never be.

Stefan Kiszko was one tragic victim of a miscarriage of justice. He was convicted of the murder of a 16-year-old girl, and spent 16 years in prison, until a campaign showed that he could not have committed the murder. The serious mistakes included the police not following up important evidence which would immediately have proved his innocence, and that three teenage girls lied in court.

The fact that miscarriages of justice can and do happen is considered by many the strongest argument against the death penalty.

THiNK about

What do you think should be the purpose of imprisoning someone?

The Difference Between Prejudice and Discrimination

Prejudice is an unfair and unreasonable opinion or feeling, especially when formed without much thought or knowledge (the word prejudice means to pre-judge). It often leads to discrimination, which has been described as "prejudice with power." Discrimination means treating a person or particular group of people differently — especially in a worse way from the way in which other people are treated — because of their skin color, sex, sexuality, disability, ethnicity, religious or other beliefs, or other attributes.

Throughout history

Prejudice and discrimination have been commonplace throughout human history. People in societies and groups have a tendency to identify with their own group. People can also be suspicious or fearful of those who belong to other groups. This can range from small groups to whole societies, and in its worst form the suspicion can become xenophobia (from two Greek words meaning "foreign" and "fear").

Changing society

In the past, discrimination was often built into laws in society. For example, in the nineteenth century, Roman Catholics weren't allowed to hold any public positions in Britain. But as social attitudes change, laws are changed, and it becomes unacceptable and unlawful to discriminate against certain groups.

You can see this most clearly in Great Britain in the way the laws relating to homosexuality have changed. Until 1967, homosexual acts between men were a criminal offense.

In 2010 in Great Britain the Equality Act was passed, and in 2013 and 2014 laws were passed in England and Wales, and Scotland, which allowed same-sex marriage. (Northern Ireland still doesn't recognize same-sex marriage.)

For much of American history, the United States had laws criminalizing homosexuality. In 2015, the Supreme Court legalized same-sex marriage.

Equality Act 2010

This UK Act of Parliament made it illegal to discriminate against anyone because of their gender, disability, race, religion or belief, sexual orientation, or age.

Hate crime has now been added to legislation, and people are encouraged to report any incidents to the police. A hate incident is "any incident which the victim, or anyone else, thinks is based on someone's prejudice towards them because of their race, religion, sexual orientation, disability or because they are transgender."

Stereotypes

A stereotype is a widely held, but inflexible and oversimplified view of a particular type of person or thing. Some stereotyping, for example, that Welsh people are good at singing, might be thought to be harmless, but sometimes the stereotype can be really damaging. For example, if a certain group of people are stereotyped as not as being as clever as everyone else, how does this affect the way that institutions treat those people? Look at the way that stereotypes affected Richard Rieser as he was growing up (pages 22-23).

How do mutual respect and tolerance work in a multi-cultural society?

How can a society balance toleration of the beliefs and practices of people from different cultures or religions living within it, when some of the practices might contradict the values expressed in the laws of that country? For example, bigamy is against the law in the US and UK, but isn't in all countries. Can you think of any other laws like this?

What's the best way of dealing with any real differences? Do we really know about different practices, or do we have a stereotyped view of the values and practices of other groups?

THINK about

Do you know someone who has experienced discrimination or prejudice? What did they do about it?

⬇ Demonstrators protest against a Russian law banning gay "propaganda." In 2017, the European court of human rights ruled that such laws were "incompatible with the notions of equality, pluralism and tolerance inherent in a democratic society."

My Experience

Richard Rieser

Richard Rieser was born in 1948. He is the managing director of World of Inclusion Ltd., a company that works to promote equality for disabled people, and an international equality trainer, consultant, filmmaker, writer, and teacher.

He told us about how his experiences of prejudice and discrimination influenced his ideas about what is right and wrong.

☀ Included and excluded

I caught polio at nine months: I lost power in the muscles of my left leg, my chest, back, and right arm. My parents were keen for me to do everything that everyone else did. I could swim, ride a bike, and walk with a limp. It was the 1950s and I was in a gang on our street, climbing trees and playing on bombsites.

The first act of discrimination against me was when the head of a primary school refused to allow me to go to his school as I was a "fire-risk." There were only three steps! This meant that I couldn't go to a school where my friends were.

☀ Experiencing prejudice

Our council, the London County Council, tried to put me into a special school for the "physically handicapped." I visited it and it reminded me of the hospital I had been in: all the children in wheelchairs, calipers etc, were sitting around doing nothing. I had a tantrum as I hated it. My parents fought for me to go a mainstream private school, paid for by the Council.

When I was 14, I transferred myself to a local secondary modern school. It was on six floors but I wasn't allowed to use the lift. The other boys bullied and taunted me because of my leg. They told me I was "ugly" and a "cripple." I believed this for years. Some staff joined in with this, especially in PE.

☀ Making sense of the world

I went to university and got a degree in Geography, and I studied for a further degree, too.

I was trying to make sense of the world: I rejected religion as I thought it was hypocritical. I realized that most of the things I had been brought up to believe in, such as patriotism and the pursuit of profits, were wrong. These created poverty and suffering throughout the world. I decided to spend time building community groups, working with trade unions and organizing in factories with working class people.

Eventually, I trained as a teacher. My needs as a disabled person weren't met – for example I was teaching in many rooms on different floors. I thought that this was my personal problem, but then I realized that disability was not "natural" but is created by society, along with discrimination against people because of their nationality, gender, race, sexuality, and poverty.

☀ Challenging discrimination

I discovered a whole history of the depiction of disability as generalized and negative: the lame boy in the "Pied Piper of Hamelin" is the only child left behind; the witch in "Hansel and Gretel" is blind and walks with a stick; the baddies in *James Bond* films are usually disabled in some way.

I came to understand that disability is a socially created oppression, which stereotypes all of us with long-term impairments instead of seeing us how we are: equal but different. This led me to develop my thinking about the need for disability equality, especially in schools.

The high point for me was representing the UK Disabled People's Movement at the United Nations. I helped draft the UN Convention on the Rights of Persons with Disabilities.

> ## "We are equal but different."

UN Convention on the Rights of Persons with Disabilities

The Convention was adopted by the United Nations in 2006. It's an international human rights treaty intended to protect the rights and dignity of persons with disabilities.

Parties to the Convention – all the countries that signed it – are required to "promote, protect, and ensure the full enjoyment of human rights by persons with disabilities, and ensure that they enjoy full equality under the law."

The Convention is helping to ensure that people with disabilities are seen as full and equal members of society, with the same human rights as everyone else.

THiNK about

What would you do if you saw a disabled person being bullied?

How Does Fairness and Unfairness Affect People?

Inequality and poverty

When we talk about inequality we are normally talking about the situation in society where some people have much more money and many more opportunities than other people. Is this situation fair? Is it fair that there are poor people in society – with little money and few possessions, while others have lots more money and many more opportunities? Not everyone would say this was unfair, so it's important to think about this.

⬆ A homeless person sleeps on the street in Paris, France.

> "... I think the best way of doing good to the poor, is not making them easy in poverty, but leading or driving them out of it."
>
> Benjamin Franklin

Is inequality bad for society?

Many people believe that it is. There are two arguments put forward for why we should narrow the gap between rich and poor in society. One is simply that huge inequalities are immoral and unjust. The parallel argument is that society should be organized to ensure "the greatest good for the greatest number." People who believe this argue that everyone in society should be cared for, that people should not be allowed to fall into dire poverty, that everyone should have access to health care, a good education and housing, and that this should be paid for through taxation, in particular a system of progressive income tax – where the wealthy are taxed at higher rates.

Some people don't agree that inequality is a problem. They oppose the redistribution of wealth through taxing the wealthy at higher rates, and agree with Benjamin Franklin, one of the founders of the United States, that giving help to the poor makes them less likely to want to work. They believe that money from the rich will always "trickle down" to the poor – for example through jobs – and that it's not the responsibility of the government to take care of the poor.

Are unequal societies "unhealthy," making them bad for everyone?

There is a great deal of evidence that the economies of very unequal societies are not "healthy," and unhealthy economies affect everyone negatively. In a purely practical way, when wealth becomes concentrated in the hands of a few people, the majority of people have little spare money to spend on everything from clothes and tech devices to going out for a meal or even buying takeout. This affects the businesses that provide the goods and services; people lose their jobs, and this makes the economy weak. People who are in the lowest-paid jobs have even less to spend on necessities, and everyone becomes poorer. So an unhealthy economy affects everyone in society.

What can be done to change the situation?

It is possible to change the inequalities in society through the policy choices made by governments, and also, on a more local scale, through supporting forms of economic democracy, where employees have a say in how an enterprise is run, and even in how profits are shared. These changes can only come about if enough people in a society decide that it's in everyone's best interests to have greater equality.

> "Homelessness and child poverty have risen, the NHS is in dire financial straits, understaffed prisons have record suicide rates, the elderly lack social care — yet the rich continue to get richer, and continue to avoid taxes. This is an expression of abject moral bankruptcy."
>
> Professors Kate Pickett and Richard Wilkinson, writing in **The Guardian** in 2017

An attempt to reduce inequality

During and after the Second World War, the government in Britain did its best to reduce inequalities. They recognized that people needed to feel that the significant burdens of the war were shared fairly by everyone. So the rationing of food, clothing, and gas affected everyone. This meant, for example, that everyone was allowed the same amount of meat, butter, and sugar. In this way the government was able to ask everyone to participate.

THiNK about

Do those who have the wealth have more power? Is that fair?

Is it people's own fault if they are poor?

Should governments provide health care, education, and housing for everyone?

How Does Inequality Affect Educational Opportunity?

Education is not just about what we learn or don't learn. It's also about how education itself is divided up into different routes and pathways. And it's about the kinds of opportunities that parents provide to enable children to "get on."

Routes through education

Here are two contrasting routes that people in the UK might take through education into life. We could say that Maria and Robert take route one while Abdul and Leanne take route two.

Route One

- **Maria and Robert are each brought up by a single parent who has had no higher education**
- can't afford preschool
- elementary and middle school
- high school
- parent gets a new job in another city, so the child must move and transfer to a new school in the middle of the school year
- "training" ie retail apprenticeship
- work in a store
- rented shared apartment
- benefits subsidizing low wages

Route Two

- **Abdul and Leanne are each born into wealth**
- preschool
- private primary (K-8) school
- private high school
- parents pay for an academic tutor
- college or university
- parents' contacts enable child to do internship with parents' support
- parents help pay off university fees and student loans
- well-paid job
- parents pay deposit on a house

Can you think of other routes, or other maps?

> " ... to educate not according to ability, but according to the social situation of the parents, is both wrong and a waste."
>
> The writer Alan Bennett, speaking at Cambridge University in 2014

Finland

Three decades ago, the government in Finland realized that their education system was seriously failing children, and they decided to make revolutionary changes, including scrapping all testing and not starting formal schooling until the age of seven. They abolished all private schools, so that everyone attends a state school, and they raised the status of teachers through higher pay and by insisting that all teachers have a Master's qualification.

There are day care programs for babies and toddlers and one year pre-school for six-year-olds, followed by nine years of compulsory comprehensive schooling. Students can then choose between an academic or a vocational track, both of which usually take three years and give a qualification to continue to tertiary education.

After years of no testing at all, Finland decided to see how their education system was doing compared to others. They joined an international testing program (called PISA – OECD Programme for International Study Assessment) and found they were at the top. They are still consistently high, but recognize that they must keep evolving.

Children in Finland attend school between the ages of seven and 15.

Fairness in education

Ideas about a fair way to run education have changed and they are different in different countries. For example, in 1944 the government for England and Wales introduced an exam at 11 called the 11-plus, which all children took. The ones who passed went to a grammar school, those that failed went to secondary modern schools. Some people also went to technical colleges. At first people thought this was fair but, by the 1960s, most people came to think it wasn't, and so the government introduced comprehensive schools.

Meanwhile, private education was never abolished and some areas kept grammar schools. Some people think this is fair. Some don't. What do you think?

THiNK
about

Find out what you can about the ideas behind the way education systems are organized in different parts of the world.

Are there fairer systems in other countries?

My Experience

Tulip Siddiq

Tulip Siddiq was born in 1982. She is the Labour Party Member of British Parliament for Hampstead and Kilburn, and was Shadow Minister for Education (Early Years) between 2016 and 2017. She has worked at Amnesty International and Save the Children on issues related to human trafficking and modern-day slavery. She told us what she thinks about injustice in society and how to combat it.

✳ Is it right to treat people well or badly because they are different in some way?

There is a lot of discrimination against people because of their skin color, their disabilities, religion, gender, and sexuality, to list the most common. In 2015/2016 there were over 169 hate-driven incidents happening in the UK every day, against people who simply look different or have different beliefs from others. For me, it's very important that people from all backgrounds work together to stop prejudice and discrimination.

To take some examples I've seen in my own life: my father uses a wheelchair. Is it right that he faces discrimination in his search for a job because of his physical disability? My mother worships at a mosque and my neighbor at a synagogue. Is it right that they have to deal with the prejudice of people who shout nasty insults at them because of their religious beliefs?

People, like myself, who work in politics, have an extra responsibility to create laws (or acts) that protect those who experience prejudice, because we represent all our constituents. One Act that I'm proud of is the Equality Act 2010 (see page 20), which protects people from discrimination in their workplace and in wider society. This Act entitles everyone, regardless of background, to the same treatment from an employer.

✳ Education is the enemy of prejudice

I believe education is the best way to stop prejudice from developing, and it also works against already established prejudice. I was lucky enough to go to good schools with broad-minded, inclusive teachers. But sadly, not everyone in the world has the same opportunities as I had or that my daughter will have.

There are other benefits to education, too. When people can read and write and discuss issues openly, they are able to understand more, and people from different backgrounds are more accepting of each other, as they learn about each other's cultures in school. Better education also means a better qualified workforce, which allows economies to flourish at home and trade peacefully with one another.

More broadly, those who can, need to work towards a world in which every child can go to school. To make this happen, we need to make sure we keep helping the poorest countries, and ensure that governments spend enough money on education to give every child the best chance of success both here and elsewhere. That will benefit us all.

✳ What else can we do?

You don't have to be a politician to help stop discrimination and prejudice. Bringing people of different faiths, belief systems, and cultures together is a really successful way of reducing prejudice. This way, people can share their cultures and reduce the likelihood of division and exclusion.

And events like the Paralympics (right) give athletes a chance to show the entire world that having a disability should be no barrier to ambition and achievement.

Opportunities for education

According to the United Nations, 61 million children of primary school age were not in school in 2016, with girls far less likely than boys to attend school.

However, things are changing. Since 2000, the United Nations says that the number of children who were out of school has fallen by almost half. This is great news. Understanding, through better schooling and education, starves ignorance and prejudice, making us all winners.

"Prejudice does not have to exist."

Is There a Right and Wrong Way to Use Language?

What part does language play in how we decide what's right and wrong? Are there right and wrong ways to use language? Should we try to control how people write and speak?

These are very complicated questions.

One example

In July 2017, the Member of Parliament Anne Marie Morris was recorded at an event using a particular expression. She said,

"Now we get to the real n----- in the woodpile, which is, in two years what happens if there is no deal?"

You'll see that we've written one of the words as "n-----." That's because the word has a history that is tied up with slavery and the idea that some people (millions, actually) could be bought, sold and forced to work. We've reached a point in most parts of the English-speaking world where we think the word is unrepeatable and yet here was an MP in 2017 using it. She apologized and the Prime Minister suspended her.

All this caused a debate in the mainstream media and on social media, too. Some people said that it showed that this MP used the expression regularly without thinking and she moved in circles where people didn't stop her to tell her it was offensive. Others said this was "over-reacting" and it was "unintentional," meaning that she didn't mean any harm to anyone.

↑ By 1860 there were four million slaves in the United States. People were bought and sold at markets like this one.

Some language "sleeps"

Part of the problem is that some unrepeatable words sit in phrases and old rhymes where they "sleep." That's to say, they're not "actively" being used to describe someone or, say, to order them to do something, which is how the word Morris said were once used. Another problem is that the word hasn't died out everywhere. For example, a good number of African-American rappers and comedians use the word, and some people feel that it is acceptable for them to use the word, but it's not acceptable for a white person to use it.

Why do you think some people say that?

Language and power – the staircase

The answer lies in the fact that such language is not "neutral," it's always used in situations which are already set up in a particular kind of way. This is what's known as the "language and power" question. Some groups of people in society tend to have more power than other groups. There are "hierarchies," arranged as on an imaginary staircase. Very few people would say we aren't all somewhere on this staircase. Where people disagree is whether we can all move up (or down) the staircase when we want to or have the ability to.

There have been arguments over the last 100 years or so about this and what are the right or wrong approaches. One part of the argument is about how we use words to describe each other.

People ask, are white people more likely to be above black people on the staircase? Are there words which not only reflect these positions but have the power to keep people lower than others? That explains why, when African-American rappers use those words, it's "ironic" – they are mocking the way people have used the word when talking to people lower down. And it's also a way of reclaiming language that was once used to abuse them.

There is the same argument about words to do with any group that experiences prejudice. People from higher up the hierarchy using these words about people lower down helps to create and consolidate the hierarchy. Some people say this use of language is not only offensive, it's using power to create prejudice and discrimination and it has to stop.

> "Language is very powerful. Language does not just describe reality. Language creates the reality it describes."
>
> **Archbishop Desmond Tutu**

THINK about

What do you think? Is it ever acceptable to use such words that have a negative history, even if that word is being "reclaimed"?

My Experience
Laura Bates

Laura Bates was born in 1986. She is the founder of the Everyday Sexism Project, which has gathered over 100,000 testimonies of gender inequality worldwide. Laura writes regularly for several publications, and also works with international groups tackling rape and abuse. We asked her what she thinks about right and wrong in society.

❊ How do ideas of what is right and wrong develop?

Most of us have firm ideas of what is right and wrong, without ever being taught them explicitly. This is especially true in relation to what's considered right and wrong for girls and boys. We've all accepted these ways of judging people depending on their gender, without ever really talking about it. These ideas are often sexist, racist, or homophobic, but we internalize them because they're all around us.

For example, we learn from children's toys (dolls for girls, engineering kits for boys) what careers are considered "suitable" before we're even old enough to walk. Girls get told they're beautiful and boys that they're big and strong. Films and television most often show men doing brave and powerful things and women looking for love or being a sidekick for a man.

❊ What effect does inequality have on people's lives?

I often hear people say that "everybody has the same chances, and if there are different outcomes to people's lives that's their fault." But the process of getting to the outcomes depends on your starting point.

If you start with fewer advantages – money, education, expectations – getting to the same outcome as someone with all the advantages is harder, if you can get there at all. There are so many obstacles along the way, including the low expectations of teachers or others, prejudice and lack of funds.

We have to remove the invisible barriers instead of placing blame on the people who are being held back by those barriers.

That goes for all sorts of different situations. For example, girls are told how to dress and behave, and not to go out alone to avoid being assaulted. This puts the onus on girls and young women, and not on those making the decision to do wrong.

So what should we do?

First, recognize that many different sorts of discrimination can be invisible. For example, many people think that sexism doesn't exist any more, and if we are white we may not see racism in action, but this doesn't mean that these problems don't exist. We must recognize the problems before we can start to solve them, so the first thing is to listen to other people's experiences.

The second challenge is to recognize all those stereotypes that sneak in without our realizing. For example, sexism in the media – when we hear about the shoes and dresses of female politicians but the policies of their male peers.

We need to campaign for politicians and businesses to make fair policies to tackle inequality and discrimination.

In the Women's March on Washington in January 2017, millions of people showed they were no longer prepared to allow sexism and inequality to continue in silence.

We should all play a part

But most of all, every one of us has to play a part if we want to change what's currently seen as normal. So, for example, if a woman is walking down the street and a man harasses her, a passerby who challenges him would send a powerful message that it's not OK. This doesn't have to involve confrontation. It might just mean offering help or support to the woman. But if we just walk on by we also send a message: this is normal and we don't have a problem with it.

It isn't enough to have strong values and keep quiet about them. We have to speak up when we see injustice, and put our values into action.

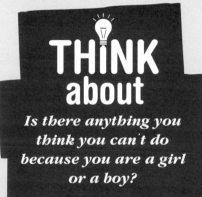

THINK about

Is there anything you think you can't do because you are a girl or a boy?

If you heard something sexist being said at school, would you try to challenge it?

"We have to speak up when we see injustice, and put our values into action."

How Does Right and Wrong Work on a Global Scale?

Pollution and climate change are global problems

There are some issues, such as pollution and climate change, that have an impact on the welfare of individuals and communities all over the world. Can the problems caused by pollution and climate change be solved by doing what is right and stopping doing what is wrong? That could be a straightforward solution if everyone agreed about what is right and wrong in these situations, but that, of course, isn't the case.

What is pollution?

Pollution is the damage caused to the environment – the water, the air, and the land around us – by harmful substances or waste. The increasing population of the world and the resultant demand on resources, and insufficient controls and laws to prevent pollution, have led to an increase in pollution.

What are climate change and global warming?

Global warming refers to the Earth's rising surface temperature, while climate change includes this warming and its effects, such as melting glaciers and the subsequent rise in sea levels, and an increase in extreme weather, leading to flooding or drought.

Global warming is one symptom of the much larger problem of climate change caused by humanity itself, resulting from the rapid increase in carbon dioxide and other greenhouse gases that affect the Earth's atmosphere. Greenhouse gases mostly result from: the burning of fossil fuels (coal, oil, and natural gas), solid waste, trees, and wood products; certain chemical reactions in manufacture; the methane emissions from livestock; and the transformation of the Earth's landscape, for instance from carbon-storing forests to farmland.

⬆ In 2017, a third of Bangladesh was affected by flooding.

How can the problems of pollution and climate change be solved?

These are huge questions and there are no simple answers. But we can only begin to solve these problems by looking at each issue in detail and then deciding what to do in each case, in fact, by deciding what is the right thing to do, and what is the wrong thing.

The only way this will be solved is through world cooperation. It's a matter of balancing different rights – for example, the rights of farmers to put pesticides on their land (polluting the water table and rivers), in order to increase their crop yields, against the rights of everyone to have clean water, free from pesticides.

There are people who say they don't believe the scientists about climate change and its effects. For example, President Donald Trump (below) supports the coal, oil, and car manufacturing industries and doesn't agree with restricting their activities.

THiNK about

Should governments ban all combustion engines, and phase in electric cars? Would that work?

If you had the power, what would you do about climate change?

Balancing harms

It's also a matter of deciding which solutions cause the least harm. For example, when governments and scientists were concentrating on climate change and looking at the effect of carbon emissions, diesel fuel for cars was encouraged because diesel produced fewer carbon emissions. But it's since become clear that diesel cars produce more pollutants which contribute to the air pollution from traffic, and that these pollutants cause serious respiratory illnesses. As a result, governments are considering a number of measures, including introducing penalties for diesel cars and banning them altogether. People who had been encouraged to buy diesel cars say that this is unfair. What should governments do?

Car manufacturers are making changes. too. For example, Volvo recently announced that it will no longer launch new car models powered only by internal combustion engines, and instead will produce only pure electric or hybrid cars, which create less pollution. Other car manufacturers are also now looking at changing over.

But will these measures happen quickly enough?

Find out

Find out what you can about different kinds of renewable energy and nuclear power. What are their advantages and disadvantages?

Is It Ever Right to Go to War?

Are all wars bad and wrong? Are some "right" or "necessary"? Who decides? These are very complex questions, and people — including philosophers, theologians, and politicians — have always argued about them. War is either offensive — when one country attacks or invades another; or defensive — when a country that has been attacked or invaded defends itself against the attacker, or helps another country that has been attacked. This might sound straightforward, but most situations are not clear-cut.

The question always comes back to fairness. Think about someone who is being bullied. Should they stand up to the bully and fight back in some way? Is that the right, or best, thing to do? Does talking work? Can arguments between two sides – even countries – be settled by discussion and negotiation?

> "War is what happens when language fails."
>
> Margaret Atwood, novelist

Was the Second World War a "necessary war"?

Most people say that it was, because of the way Hitler's Germany (see page 17) and its allies behaved.

The causes of the war are complex, and go back to the aftermath of Germany's defeat in the First World War. Under the Treaty of Versailles, Germany lost territory to pay for the damage caused by the war. This caused resentment among the German people, as it brought hardship to many. In the early 1930s, the Nazi Party's Adolf Hitler (see page 17) was voted into power after he promised to rip up the hated Treaty. Hitler's program of retaking lost territory started in 1936 when German troops entered the Rhineland. This was followed by invasions into Sudetenland in Czechoslovakia.

Britain and France did not want to start another war, so they accepted Hitler's assurances that he would stop there. But he didn't. In 1939, he invaded the rest of Czechoslovakia. Still, Britain and France were not prepared to take military action, but they did promise that if Germany invaded Poland they would. This happened in September 1939. Britain and France were then at war with Germany.

Find out

Find out what you can about Hitler and the Nazis, and their actions, both before the war started and during the war. Do you think it was right to go to war against them?

What if someone disagrees with a war?

According to the UN Convention on Human Rights, a conscientious objector is an "individual who has claimed the right to refuse to perform military service on the grounds of freedom of thought, conscience, or religion." The Convention upholds this principle, and supports laws allowing objectors to be exempted from military service altogether, or to serve either as non-combatants or in civilian services.

There wasn't always such a humane attitude, and conscientious objectors have been imprisoned and even executed at different times in history.

The United Nations

The United Nations has discussed and passed many resolutions on issues related to war, invasions, and occupations. And in international law it's illegal to invade a country purely and only in order to change the government ("regime change").

A controversial action?

In 2003, the USA and Britain invaded Iraq. They did so to oust Saddam Hussein (regime change) and his government. They claimed that Iraq had "weapons of mass destruction" and this was sufficient reason. This was never proved and they didn't wait for a second UN resolution before taking action. According to UN statutes, this was an illegal act.

Muhammad Ali, conscientious objector

Muhammad Ali, the American boxer and activist (below), in 1966 refused to be conscripted into the armed forces because he was opposed to the Vietnam War. He was denied a boxing license and was stripped of his passport and heavyweight title; the case against him was overturned on appeal after four years.

THiNK about

If your country went to war, under what circumstances would you take part?

Find out how people have resisted invasions and occupations. If your country was invaded, under what circumstances would you resist?

How Do Children Learn about Right and Wrong?

Dos and Don'ts

If you are someone under 18 reading this page, the chances are that the life you lead is full of rules (dos and don'ts), with punishments, sanctions and words of "rebuke" (ie being told off) if you break them.

It's obvious that for the very first years of your life, if you don't like any of this, there's nothing you can do about it apart from shout – which we've all seen babies and toddlers do very often!

Can you question the rules?

As we get older things change. We start to have all sorts of ideas about right and wrong that might not be exactly the same as our parents' and carers'. These might be to do with, for example, what you're allowed to do (bedtimes, going out, what kinds of friends you have, etc). They might be about the kinds of punishments you get when you break the rules. They can also be about who makes up the rules and whether you get a say in things.

Now let's switch to school. Some of the rules and punishments are similar but some are different, especially to do with when it's not right to talk, when not to get up and walk around, what kinds of punishments are given out for disobeying the rules (being sent to see the principal, detentions, suspensions, exclusions, etc).

Pupil Referral Units

In the UK, young people who don't or can't abide by the rules might be excluded from mainstream school and sent to a Pupil Referral Unit (PRU). These have been designed to provide education for children who are excluded, sick, or for other reasons are unable to attend a mainstream or special school. So, they are not only for children who have been excluded from school because of their behavior, although many of them are what is called "challenging." The best PRUs treat every child as an individual and work with them to help them learn, and enjoy learning.

"It takes time – you have to be there, listen to them rant and so on. The bottom line is trust."… We "increased attendance by 30 percent by creating an environment where pupils want to be. Every day they come in because the experience is a positive one – they feel welcomed and it's safe."

Tony Meehan, head teacher of Latimer Alternative Provision Academy

Ideas about punishments change

One debate that has taken place many times in the last 50 years is over the physical punishment of children. For example, when Michael Rosen was nine years old in 1955, he booed a teacher in the school playground and was caned with a stick for "disobedience." In 1986, physical punishment of school children by teachers was banned by the UK government in state-run schools. In the United States, there are 19 states where it is still legal to use corporal, or physical, punishment in public schools. Meanwhile a debate goes on as to whether governments should pass a law banning parents and carers from hitting children. There are already laws that ban physical punishment in the home as well as at school in nearly 50 countries.

THiNK about

Some people say that governments are right to abolish physical or corporal punishment in order to protect children. Others argue that it should be nothing to do with government, and should always be the decision of the parents and schools themselves. What do you think?

Find out

See what you can find out about what happens to children under 18 who not only break the rules at school, but also break the law.

➡ This illustration from the 1880s shows how children used to be hit on the hand with a cane as a punishment for disobedience.

My Experience
Alex Wheatle

The writer Alex Wheatle was born in 1963 and spent most of his childhood in a Surrey, England, children's home. He received a short prison sentence following the Brixton uprising of 1981. In prison, and after his release, he wrote poems and lyrics, becoming known as the Brixton Bard. He won the 2016 Guardian Children's Fiction Prize and was nominated for the Carnegie Medal in 2016 and 2017. We asked Alex how his experiences have influenced his values and his ideas of what is right and wrong.

❊ What effect did your treatment in the children's home have on you?

When I was three I was sent into the Shirley Oaks care home. It was a place of nightmares, where certain adults physically, sexually, and mentally abused children with impunity. To be told your parents abandoned you like you're a bag of rubbish – you believe it. It affects your whole worldview.

Before the age of 18, I felt worthless, and because of this I sabotaged every opportunity I had at school and further education. I was excellent at cricket and was once offered the chance to be captain of the school cricket team. I declined. I shied away from any kind of responsibility. I saw value in others, but not in myself.

Growing up, my notion of right and wrong was confused. I was fulfilling the very worst expectations I had of myself.

❊ How did you develop a sense of self worth?

As a teenager, I struggled with anger and trust issues, left school with no qualifications, slipped into petty crime and then landed in prison for five months following the 1981 Brixton uprising.

The only way I could access love and see value in myself was when someone else did. This gateway happened in prison, when I wrote poems about my life in care. My cell-mate said "That's very good." He was a Rastafarian and had a tremendous belief in himself. The recognition from those poems and the self-worth that followed led me, finally, to believe that I could contribute to society.

Sharing a small space with another person meant I had to consider someone else's space and feelings. I slowly came to realize that other people had difficult experiences too, and I wanted to write about their backgrounds and traumas.

⋇ What do you think prisons should be for?

I believe that we can help people to develop and change, so we should rehabilitate, not just punish. I came out of prison determined to do something with my life. I began to read greedily and I trained as an engineer. I was also keeping a diary, writing song lyrics and poetry.

⋇ Can reading make a difference?

Reading fiction builds empathy. I believe this very strongly. I started to devour books and empathized with the characters. I think that if young people involved in knife crime read stories, they would begin to see themselves in other children, empathy would grow and they would consider laying down their knives. Schools could encourage this.

⋇ How has being a father changed you?

The biggest impact on me was becoming a father at twenty. My own lack of love as a child drove me – I was determined that any child of mine would have love.

It's wrong to look on any set of children and see some as failures, or potential failures. We need to build esteem and to help all children develop emotionally, as well as educating them intellectually.

We need to reassess the notion of failure. Children are living with stress levels we haven't seen before. Social media highlights what the elites are doing, wearing, what they own. The pressures are on children to do or have the same.

Parents need the support of school and society to help them instil their children with belief in themselves. It is a challenge.

⋇ All children should be seen as having equal value and worth

We should be educating all children from a young age that every individual has worth. Society's expectations of those children in care or from poor homes are the lowest. This is wrong.

The poorest child's life should be seen as just as valuable as that of a prince or princess.

THiNK about

Do you believe there is good in everybody?

Alex asks you to think about whether you would have seen the good in him when he was a wild eighteen-year-old boy.

" I was determined that any child of mine would have love."

41

How Disasters Make Us Question What's Right and Wrong

*A*s we all know, every so often there are disasters: floods, fires, traffic pile-ups, gas explosions, and many more terrible events. These raise important questions about right and wrong.

- Was the disaster really "natural" or is there at least some part of it for which people are responsible? Or was it perhaps entirely the result of human error or irresponsibility? If it could have been avoided, why wasn't it? Was it anything to do with not enough money or care being spent on safety or prevention?

- If there are aspects to it for which people are responsible, does this mean that any of the following are at fault (i.e. "wrong"): one person, several people, the "authorities" (this often means the local government), a company, several companies, a minister, a government department?

- If people are at fault, what should happen? Should they be brought to court? If they are brought to court is there a fair trial? If they are found guilty, what should happen to them? Does this happen?

- Immediately following the disaster, were things done properly? If not, why not? Was this anything to do with money or crisis management? Who should have done things properly?

- As time goes on, are the victims of the disaster treated well or badly? Why? Was this anything to do with money? Who should have been looking after those affected? What is the right way to treat victims of a disaster?

- Who behaved well? Should they be rewarded? Does the way they behaved offer any pointers as to how we might all behave in ordinary times?

Think about

Research a disaster that has happened locally or anywhere in the world and think about how the points were dealt with. Some international examples are:

The Bhopal disaster – gas leak at the Union Carbide India Ltd pesticide plant in Bhopal, Madhya Pradesh, in India in 1984.

Hurricane Katrina – the extremely destructive tropical storm that hit the Gulf Coast of the United States in 2005.

The Exxon Valdez disaster – the 1989 oil spill from the oil tanker Exxon Valdez that caused what is considered to be one of the most devastating human-caused environmental disasters.

The Grenfell Tower fire

All these issues came up after a disaster that happened in West London in June 2017.

There was a fire at a tower block in which 71 people are known to have died. The fire ran through the whole block – Grenfell Tower – and everyone had to leave their homes. It was one of the worst fire disasters that has ever happened in the UK.

Immediately, the survivors started asking some of the questions on the list on page 42. And this was followed up by commentators in the media.

People wanted to know things like:

- How did the fire start?
- Was there anything in how the building was made which meant that the fire spread so quickly?
- Were there combustible materials in the building that were chosen because they were cheaper?
- Had the council listened to the people living in the block when they had raised concerns about fire safety?
- Had the authorities taken note of what had happened when fires in other tower blocks broke out? If not, why not?
- Did the fire service have all the right equipment to fight the fire and rescue people? If not, why not?
- Were the survivors treated properly? Were they found places to stay straightaway? Were they found long-term places to stay within reach of the community? If not, why not?

It was immediately clear that many of the survivors, people in the neighborhood, and the survivors' families, did all they could to help anyone in difficulty. Some commentators said that this showed the "good" side to people, that human beings have this quality of being able to be kind, to help and cooperate for the general good.

Does a disaster like the Grenfell Tower fire make us think about our values more closely? Do people responding to a disaster act consciously according to their values or do they act spontaneously?

⬆ Volunteers sort donations of food and clothing to help people who had to flee their homes in the wake of the Grenfell Tower fire.

What Are Your Values?

*T*his book raises questions to do with right and wrong, and asks you to come up with opinions and thoughts of your own. Perhaps you did this as you read it, or while you discussed it with others.

Always keep in mind that right and wrong can be very complex. And it's the questions we ask ourselves that are often just as important as the answers. Questions can prompt discussion which can lead to change.

Did you change your mind?

While you were reading, thinking and talking, did you change your mind about anything? Why was that? Do you think there's anything you've read, or any conversation you've had about what you've read, that will make you behave differently or do something new? Why is that?

Several people in the book have talked about what might be called their "core values." That's the main principles which guide them in their daily lives, their work, the way they vote or the kinds of clubs, societies, or religious institutions they belong to.

The Golden Rule

Remember the Golden Rule that we mentioned early on? One example of it that you may have heard is "Love thy neighbour." People usually take this to mean "be good and kind and caring to the person nearest to you." And in turn, this has been taken to mean that if we all do that, society as a whole – and indeed the world – will get better.

What do you think of this principle? Would it work? Why might it not work? Can you think of a better principle?

"The strongest democracies flourish from frequent and lively debate, but they endure when people of every background and belief find a way to set aside smaller differences in service of a greater purpose."

Barack Obama

THiNK
about

What principles and values do you think can best convey your own ideas about right and wrong?

Your "volcano bag"

To help you make a list of the values that are important to you, you could think of this: there was a volcano (above) on the island of Montserrat in the Caribbean. Many people had to leave the island when it erupted. One woman who stayed was asked what she would do if she heard the volcano rumbling. She said that she had a "volcano bag" hanging by her front door. In the bag were the things that mattered to her most: souvenirs from her family, and from her own life.

You could say that we all have a mental volcano bag: the important things that we carry with us which guide us through life – especially for when our personal volcano blows up. The people in Grenfell Tower and nearby experienced something just like that. And in their mental "volcano bag" they had something like "help each other" as a basic "right thing to do."

You could talk or write about what you think is in your own mental volcano bag.

> **"Democratic dissent is not disloyalty, it is a positive civic duty."**
> Shami Chakrabarti

What can we do to bring about what we believe is right?

Much harder, but just as necessary, is the question, "What can we, as individuals or as members of a society or community, do to change those things we see as wrong or unjust?"

We know that in every corner and walk of life, in every place of work, there are problems. This is just another way of saying that the question of right and wrong crops up everywhere.

But what do we do about these things? Moan to ourselves? Complain to others in the hope that they will do something? Write a letter to the person you think is responsible, or to the newspaper or television program? Go to see your local representative, a lawyer, or a religious person? Do you take part by joining an association, an organization, a protest group, or a political party?

If you live in the United States you'll know that you can do any of these things and they might have the result you want. In some countries you're not allowed to do these things. Some problems are bigger than just our neighborhood or even our country – things like climate change.

THiNK about

How do you think we should tackle the things in society that we see as wrong or unjust?

45

apartheid the former political system in South Africa, based on racial segregation, in which only white people had full political rights and others, especially black people, were forced to live separately with inferior facilities

carbon emissions the carbon dioxide produced by cars (and by planes and factories etc), which is harmful to the environment

civic life people's public life concerned with the affairs of the community or country, in contrast to their personal life

civil rights rights designed to protect individuals from unfair treatment and to ensure they receive equal treatment, free from discrimination

communism a political system in which all property is owned and controlled by all the members of a community and everyone works as much as they can and receives what they need

conscription the process of forcing someone by law to serve in one of the armed forces

constitution the set of political principles and rights – usually written – by which a state or organization is governed, especially in relation to the rights of the people it governs

democracy a system of government based on the belief in freedom and equality between people, in which power is either held by elected representatives or directly by the people themselves

dictator a leader of a country, who has not been elected by the people and who has complete power

discrimination treating a person or particular group of people differently – usually unfavorably – because of their skin color, sex, sexuality, etc

elite the most powerful, and usually the richest and best-educated, group in a society

empathize to be able to understand how someone else feels

feminism the belief that women should be allowed the same rights, power, and opportunities as men and be treated in the same way

global warming Earth's rising surface temperature and its effects, such as melting glaciers and the subsequent rise in sea levels

humanists people who believe that people's spiritual and emotional needs can be met without following a god or religion

hybrid cars cars that can run on either electricity or gas

justice fairness in the way people are dealt with, often in relation to the law

justice system the system in a society in which people who are accused of crimes are judged in a court of law

pragmatism a practical approach to dealing with problems in a way that suits the conditions that actually exist, rather than following fixed ideas or rules

prejudice an unreasonable and unfair opinion about a person or group, especially when formed without enough thought or knowledge

revolution a change in the political system of a country, often brought about by violence or war

rule of law a set of laws that people in a society must obey

tertiary education education at college or university level

theologians people who study religion and religious belief

tolerance a willingness to accept behavior and beliefs that are different from your own, even if you do not agree with or approve of them

United Nations (UN) an international organization that was established in 1945 and aims to solve world problems in a peaceful way. UN resolutions are an official decision voted on by the UN

universal adult suffrage the right for all adults to vote with no restriction by race, sex, belief, wealth, or social status

Further Information

Here are some books and websites you might find interesting:

Books

Everyday Sexism, and *Girl Up* by Laura Bates (Simon and Schuster)

Liccle Bit, *Crongton Knights*, and *Straight Outta Crongton* by Alex Wheatle (Little, Brown)

The Panchatantra by Vishnu Sharma (Penguin Books)

Aesop's Fables by Michael Rosen (Tradewind)

The Wrong Side of Right by Jenn Marie Thorne (Dial)

Young Citizen's Passport (England and Wales, Northern Ireland, and Scotland) published by the Citizenship Foundation

The Story of Ruby Bridges by Robert Coles (Scholastic)

The Island by Armin Greder (Allen and Unwin)

Noughts and Crosses by Malorie Blackman (Corgi)

The Trap, *Raining Fire*, and *End Game* by Alan Gibbons (Orion Children's Books)

The Little Book of Thunks by Ian Gilbert (Crown House Publishing)

Websites

The Citizenship Foundation http://www.citizenshipfoundation.org.uk. They say:

"We help young people to understand the law, politics and democratic life... We want society to be fairer, more inclusive and more cohesive. We want a democracy in which everyone has the knowledge, skills, and confidence to take part as effective citizens."

openDemocracy https://www.opendemocracy.net. They say:

"Through reporting and analysis of social and political issues, openDemocracy seeks to challenge power and encourage democratic debate across the world. With human rights as our central guiding focus, we ask tough questions about freedom, justice and democracy."

Amnesty International https://www.amnesty.org. They say:

"We work to protect women, men and children wherever justice, freedom, truth and dignity are denied. As a global movement of over 7 million people, Amnesty International is the world's largest grassroots human rights organisation. We investigate and expose abuses, educate and mobilise the public, and help transform societies to create a safer, more just world. We received the Nobel Peace Prize for our life-saving work."

How to get involved

Once you have decided on your personal values, you might want to think about how you could express these values. You could join the youth section of an organization such as a political party or a pressure group that campaigns for issues you are interested in. Or closer to home, you could join the student council at your school.

Published in 2018 by The Rosen Publishing Group, Inc.
29 East 21st Street, New York, NY 10010

First Edition

Library of Congress Cataloging-in-Publication Data

Names: Rauf, Don, author.
Title: Thomas Paine : author of Common sense / Don Rauf.
Description: New York : Rosen Publishing Group, Inc., 2018. | Series: Spotlight on civic courage: heroes of conscience | Includes bibliographical references and index. | Audience: Grades 5–10.
Identifiers: LCCN 2017013073| ISBN 9781538381007 (library bound) | ISBN 9781538380970 (pbk.) | ISBN 9781538380987 (6 pack)
Subjects: LCSH: Paine, Thomas, 1737-1809—Juvenile literature. | Political scientists—United States—Biography—Juvenile literature. |Revolutionaries—United States—Biography—Juvenile literature. | United States—History—Revolution, 1775–1783—Juvenile literature.
Classification: LCC JC178.V5 R38 2017 | DDC 320.51092 [B] —dc23
LC record available at https://lccn.loc.gov/2017013073

Manufactured in the United States of America

On the cover: This portrait of Thomas Paine is based on an earlier portrait of the writer that was painted by George Romney. In the background is the first volume of the *Pennsylvania Magazine*, which Paine edited in 1775 and 1776.

CONTENTS

America's Unsung Hero

Benjamin Franklin once said that Thomas Paine was more responsible for the creation of the United States than "any other living person on the continent." While George Washington won victories on the battlefield, Paine won the hearts and minds of Americans. His published work *Common Sense* inspired citizens to fight for independence during the American Revolution. When colonists needed encouragement, they turned to Paine's words to strengthen their courage. In other essays, he took a bold stand against monarchies and spoke on behalf of the common man despite strong opposition to his efforts.

Paine's writing spurred people to action in the name of freedom and equality—not just in the United States but also in England and France. "Where liberty is not, there is my country," he said. When he died, Paine's contributions to America had been largely forgotten. Still, his ideas about equal rights and opportunities for all citizens would live on. His words had great power that would stir generations to come.

Thomas Paine showed the power of the written word. Though Paine might not be as well-known as some of the other founding fathers are today, his published works inspired Americans in their fight for independence.

GROWING UP WITH INEQUALITY

Thomas Paine was born in Thetford, England, north of London, on February 9, 1737. He grew up among farmers and people of modest means. His father was a Quaker corset maker. As a Quaker, he believed in the equality of all human beings and social justice. At the time, wealthy families controlled the government. Property owners were the only people allowed to vote and run for office. The poor often turned to crime to survive, but petty offenses, such as shoplifting, could be punishable by death—a fact Paine often confronted since his family home faced the gallows. Young Paine found the privileges of the rich and treatment of the poor to be unfair.

Paine's parents paid for him to attend grammar school for five years. When he was twelve, however, he left school and continued learning on his own. To make sure he could earn a living, his father taught him the corset-making trade.

In eighteenth century England, petty crimes such as stealing food could be punishable by hanging. Growing up near the gallows, Paine developed outrage at the injustices directed toward the lower classes.

HARDSHIPS AS A YOUNG ADULT

In his late teens, Paine took off to London to pursue adventure. He wanted to work aboard a privateer (a vessel authorized by the government to capture enemy merchant ships). Paine's father, however, convinced him to stick with corset making. He remained in London, working among the poor, who were constantly rioting over elections, food, workhouses, and other issues.

At age twenty, privateer work still called to him. Although the job was dangerous, he left corset making behind for a job at sea. In less than a year, he made enough money to devote time exclusively to reading and attending lectures on math, science, and astronomy.

By many accounts, Paine's looks did him no favors. One biography said he had a long nose and a "blazing red face dotted with purple blotches." His blue eyes, however, were full of fire. Despite his appearance, he won the heart of Mary Lambert. After they married in 1759, she became pregnant, but Mary and the baby died during childbirth.

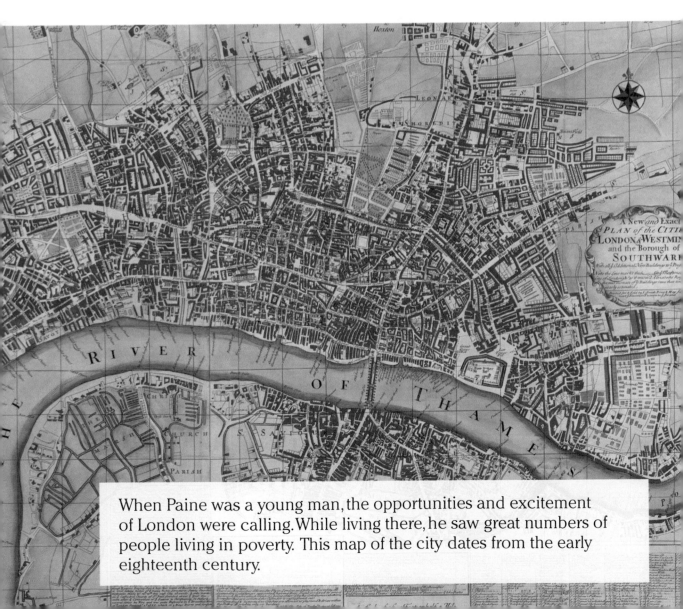

When Paine was a young man, the opportunities and excitement of London were calling. While living there, he saw great numbers of people living in poverty. This map of the city dates from the early eighteenth century.

EARLY POLITICAL PUBLISHING

After Mary died, Paine gained a new job as an excise tax collector. These government workers collected a tax on imported goods, such as tea, coffee, tobacco, and alcohol.

In 1771, at age thirty-four, Paine married the twenty-one-year-old Elizabeth Ollive. They settled in Lewes, where he also ran her father's tobacco shop part-time. In his spare time, he wrote for local newspapers and joined the Headstrong Club, a group of pub-goers who debated politics. He developed a reputation for political knowledge and argument. When fellow excise collectors turned to Paine to help gain higher pay, he published his first political work in 1772 in defense of

a wage increase. Paine distributed four thousand copies to Parliament members and others. The Excise Board may have been wary of Paine's talents of persuasion and fired him. Soon after losing the job, the tobacco shop went bankrupt and his wife left him. Paine would never remarry. He left Lewes looking for a fresh start.

- 1774. IN THIS HOUSE. LIVED THOMAS PAINE. WRITER AND REVOLUTIONARY

While residing in the Bull House at Lewes with his second wife, Paine honed his skills at argument and writing, publishing a defense of a wage increase for tax collectors.

A Fateful Meeting with Benjamin Franklin

At this low point, Paine had a fortunate turn. An excise collector friend introduced him to Benjamin Franklin, who was visiting London in his role as spokesperson for the American colonies. An author, scientist, postmaster, politician, and diplomat, Franklin was famous for his wide-ranging knowledge. Franklin recognized Paine's intelligence and passion to succeed. He advised him to move to America and gave him letters of introduction.

In fall 1774, at age thirty-seven, Paine set sail with Franklin's personal endorsement in hand. Crowded trans-Atlantic ships were notorious for spreading disease, and Paine became horribly sick with typhus during his journey. When he arrived in the colonies, he established himself in Philadelphia. As Paine regained his health in a rented room in the heart of the city, he looked for new opportunity in the thriving economic center. Philadelphia, which at this time was the largest city in colonial America, would transform his life.

After a streak of bad luck, Paine had a life-changing meeting with Benjamin Franklin. Franklin recognized Paine's potential, gave him letters of recommendation, and set him on course to a future in America.

PAINE FINDS HIS VOICE

In Philadelphia, Paine met the printer Robert Aitken, who hired him to be the editor of *The Pennsylvania Magazine*. From February 1775 to May 1776, he edited articles and churned out political analyses and essays on serious topics.

In July of 1775, Paine published a poem about the Liberty Tree. Defiant colonists gathered beneath this striking elm near Boston Common to share ideas and protest against British policies. British troops cut the elm to the ground. Afterward, hundreds of towns in every colony planted liberty trees or set up liberty poles flying flags with the liberty tree image. Paine's poem helped the tree become an international symbol of the fight for liberty:

> From the East to the West blow the trumpet to arms,
> Thro' the land let the sound of it flee;
> Let the far and the near all unite with a cheer,
> In defense of our Liberty Tree.

As the editor of the *Pennsylvania Magazine* Paine wrote many social commentaries, including a poem about Boston's famed Liberty Tree. This sketch shows the Liberty Tree soon before it was cut down by the British.

A Call for Independence

Paine arrived in the colonies at a time when resentment against England was growing. England had been taxing the colonists, but many Americans felt this unfair because they had no representation in British government. As tensions mounted, many Americans advocated for total independence. Other colonists, however, were still devoted to the mother country and doubting the bloody cost of war.

Paine knew he could help the push for independence by swaying hearts and minds. On January 9, 1776, he published *Common Sense*, a rallying cry to break with England. He produced it anonymously because it could be seen as an act of treason.

Common Sense faulted the British government for being run by kings and aristocrats who inherited power. Paine called for a democratic government—in which the people ruled. He made the case that America did not depend on England economically and that it had the human and natural resources to build its own military.

George III was the king of Great Britain during the American Revolution. During his reign, the British Parliament passed laws taxing the colonists without giving them fair representation in the government.

COMMON SENSE;

ADDRESSED TO THE

INHABITANTS

OF

AMERICA,

On the following interesting

SUBJECTS.

I. Of the Origin and Design of Government in general, with concise Remarks on the English Constitution.

II. Of Monarchy and Hereditary Succession.

III. Thoughts on the present State of American Affairs.

IV. Of the present Ability of America, with some miscellaneous Reflections.

Man knows no Master save creating HEAVEN,
Or those whom choice and common good ordain.
THOMSON.

PHILADELPHIA;

Printed, and Sold, by R. BELL, in Third-Street,

MDCCLXXVI.

Paine wrote, "Everything that is right or natural pleads for separation … Even the distance at which the Almighty hath placed England and America, is a strong and natural proof that the authority of the one over the other was never the design of heaven." He went on, "The cause of America is in a great measure the cause of all mankind … We have it in our power to begin the world over again."

Paine's language appealed to common people, expressing an anger that many were feeling. By April 1776, about 120,000 copies were in circulation. George Washington, Thomas Jefferson, and John Adams praised it. Copies were translated into different languages and circulated throughout Europe. The document paved the way for the Declaration of Independence, which Congress approved on July 4, 1776.

Thomas Paine now knew his mission in life—to write and champion the fight for liberty, wherever that might be.

Published in January 1776, months before the Declaration of Independence, Paine's *Common Sense* persuaded many colonists that America needed to break with Great Britain and become its own nation.

TIMES THAT TRY MEN'S SOULS

By fall 1776, the British had made decisive victories in their fight against the colonies, including the capture of New York City. Between September and December, eleven thousand American volunteers quit. During a frigid December, Washington and his troops camped in Pennsylvania, across the Delaware River across from Trenton, New Jersey, which was controlled by the British. With morale low, Washington needed Paine's words to inspire the troops. On December 19, 1776, Paine rushed to publish *The American Crisis*, the first of thirteen essays supporting a self-governing America.

When copies reached Washington's camp, he read the stirring words to his men: "THESE are the times that try men's souls … Tyranny, like hell, is not easily conquered; yet we have this consolation with us, that the harder the conflict, the more glorious the triumph."

The troops crossed the Delaware on Christmas night, catching the enemy off guard and winning the Battle of Trenton. Paine's words had lifted the troops and helped turn the tide toward American victory.

By Christmas 1776, General Washington and his men were disheartened after losing several battles. Paine's *The American Crisis*, however, helped inspire them to cross the Delaware River and defeat the British forces.

SERVING A NEW NATION

Starting in 1777, Paine served as secretary of the Committee of Foreign Affairs for two years. He then took a position as a clerk with the state of Pennsylvania's legislative body. Before the American Revolution ended, Paine also raised money to help pay for soldiers' wages and supplies. He published several works, including *Public Good* in 1780, which called for a strong central government under a continental constitution.

As the war drew to an end in 1783, Paine published his final *Crisis* pamphlet on April 19. He wrote, "The times that tried men's souls are over—and the greatest and completest revolution the world ever knew is gloriously and happily accomplished."

At the end of the war, Paine was looking for a cause and a way to earn money. Fortunately, Washington rewarded him with a sum of cash and a 300-acre (121 hectare) farm in New Rochelle, New York, allowing him to live comfortably for the rest of his life.

Throughout the Revolution, Paine championed the fight for independence, writing thirteen *American Crisis* pamphlets. For his efforts, Washington awarded him a sum of cash and this cottage in New Rochelle, New York.

RIGHTS OF MAN

In 1787, Paine returned to Europe, splitting his time between London and Paris. In France resentment and resistance were building against King Louis XVI, who had imposed heavy taxes on the poor. On July 14, 1789, the French Revolution began as the lower classes fought to overthrow the monarchy and bring equality to all citizens. The revolt became chaotic and bloody, as "enemies" of the new movement were put to death.

Warning of the dangers of public revolt, Paine's friend Edmund Burke wrote *Reflections on the Revolution in France*. In response, Paine wrote the *Rights of Man*. Published in two parts in 1791 and 1792, it argued that breaking away from a monarchy was a just course that all men should pursue. ("Hereditary succession is a

burlesque.") He said that early violence in the French Revolution came from the example set by the monarchy and would settle down. He expressed his support for a government with free education, unemployment benefits, old-age pensions, and public housing.

Parisians stormed the Bastille prison on July 14, 1789, signaling the start of the French Revolution and the fight to overthrow the King Louis XVI and the ruling aristocracy.

This British cartoon depicts Paine as a radical who wrote *Rights of Man* to defend the French Revolution and appeal to the English to overthrow their monarchy and organize a republic.

Rights of Man became a bigger blockbuster than *Common Sense*, selling 1.5 million copies—more than any book in English history other than the Bible. The work became required reading for political clubs across England. It called for wider representation in government since only male landowners could vote at the time.

The British government worried that Paine's words might spread the disease of revolution from France to England. The book was officially banned. Those who printed or sold Paine's work were punished. English aristocrats wore shoe nails inscribed with the initials "TP" so they could symbolically crush Paine's ideas with each step. The government spread rumors to disgrace Paine and paint him as dangerous. People were incited to riot, burning effigies of Paine along with his books. Paine was charged with treason. But before he could be tried and fearing for his life, he sailed from England to France on September 14, 1792.

FROM FRENCH HERO TO ENEMY

Upon landing in France, Paine received a hero's welcome. He was greeted with cheers of "*Vive Thomas Paine!*" The newly formed French government took inspiration from his belief in equality and democracy. It adopted the Declaration of the Rights of Man and of the Citizen, a statement of principles endorsing equal opportunity, freedom of speech, and a representative government. Within two weeks of his arrival, Paine became a French citizen and government representative. Back in England, meanwhile, a jury found him guilty of sedition.

During Paine's first few weeks in France, the governing body (called the National Convention) formally abolished the monarchy and established the new republic. King Louis XVI was put on trial and found guilty of treason. Paine rallied to save his life, arguing that "as France has been the first of European nations to abolish royalty, let her also be the first to abolish the punishment of death."

Passed by France's newly formed government in 1789, the Declaration of the Rights of Man and of the Citizen echoed the principles of liberty and equality advocated by Thomas Paine.

When Maximilien Robespierre took control in France, he started the Reign of Terror, executing thousands, including King Louis XVI and Marie Antoinette, pictured here. Paine himself narrowly escaped the guillotine.

Maria Antoinetta Dronning af Frankerige Henrettes den

Paine warned that executing the king would make enemies for the new republic, which would lose support from the United States since the king had supported the American Revolution. Still, the National Convention decided on death, sending both Louis and his queen, Marie Antoinette, to the guillotine.

By summer 1793, turmoil in the new democratic French government led to the rise of a dictatorship led by Maximilien Robespierre. He began the Reign of Terror, executing thousands suspected of opposing the government. Paine was no longer a hero but an enemy who had called to save the king's life. On December 28, 1793, he was imprisoned and became seriously sick with typhoid fever. He was scheduled to be executed, but an error at the prison spared his life. After Robespierre was overthrown, James Monroe (the US minister to France and later a US president) pled for his release. Paine left a free man after ten months in jail.

THE AGE OF REASON

Before his imprisonment in 1793, Paine completed the first part of *The Age of Reason*. It was a critique of organized religion, which he thought was based on superstition and could often become corrupt with power. His view of life was increasingly based on science and reason.

The Age of Reason, however, also rejected atheism. Although Paine had problems with organized religion, he saw how rejection of the church in the French Revolution could lead to losing a sense of what is right and wrong.

Paine considered himself a "deist," one who believed in God but not as practiced in churches. He explained, "I believe in one God, and no more ... My own mind is my own church." He once wrote: "My religion is to do good."

For most readers of the time, *The Age of Reason* went too far. The British government prosecuted those who sold and distributed it. In America, the work caused many to view Paine as godless and too radical.

In 1794, Paine criticized institutionalized religions in *The Age of Reason*. He advocated for deism, a belief that God exists, but the world runs according to scientific and rational principles.

A MIND FOR INVENTION

In addition to writing, Paine had a passion for science. During the American Revolution, he devoted time to designing a tool that would hurl firebombs but never finished the project. After the war, he created a "smokeless candle," a crane for lifting heavy objects, and a motor powered by exploding gunpowder.

Paine had a fascination with bridges, especially those constructed of iron because they would withstand the battering of water, ice, and wind. He tried to raise funds to build an iron bridge over the Harlem River in New York City in 1785 and for one over the Seine in Paris the following year, but they never came to be. In 1796, however, his plan for a

φ SML 1972

single-span bridge in Wearmouth, England, was completed. The iron bridge stretched 240 feet (73 meters) across the Wear River without any supports along its span from end to end. At the time, it was the longest single-span bridge in the world. It was taken down in 1927.

Throughout his life, Paine maintained an interest in the world of science. He created several inventions and designed a few bridges, including the iron Wearmouth Bridge, pictured here.

Coming Back to America

U pon Thomas Jefferson's invitation, the sixty-five-year-old Paine returned to the United States in 1802. As the new century began, Paine's earlier patriotic writing had been largely forgotten. Many people viewed him as a troublemaker. Christians regarded him as godless. Nevertheless, Paine would not be silenced. He wrote articles criticizing the Federalist Party of Alexander Hamilton as a danger to democracy and for promoting war, debt, taxes, and lies. In 1805, four years before his death, Paine praised America's original fight for independence: "It was the opportunity of beginning the world anew, as it were;

and of bringing forward a new system of government in which the rights of all men should be preserved."

On June 8, 1809, Paine died in Greenwich Village, New York, at the age of seventy-three. Only six mourners attended his funeral. His obituary in the *New York Citizen* noted, "He had lived long, did some good and much harm."

This simple plaque in New Rochelle marks Paine's original burial site. While only six people attended his funeral, his words have lived on to inspire many future generations.

INSPIRATION FOR WORKERS AND WOMEN

Throughout the nineteenth century, the workers' rights movements in England and America turned to Thomas Paine's writings. Those fighting for better conditions would read *Rights of Man* in secret or at union meetings, where some would sing (to the tune of "My Country, Tis of Thee") "God save great Thomas Paine, His Rights of Man explain, to every soul." Paine's works were said to influence the voting rights movement as well, leading to the 1867 Reform Bill in England, expanding the vote to about 1.5 million men. (British women would have to wait until 1918.)

In 1819, the English journalist William Cobbett dug up Paine's body and brought his remains back to England. He intended to build a memorial to rally the democracy movement there but the project stalled.

In America in the 1830s, the Scottish-born writer, lecturer, and activist Fanny Wright fought for women's rights. Wright's father had circulated the works of Thomas Paine, and she gained a reputation as being the "female Thomas Paine" because of her struggle for equality.

The journalist William Cobbett was such a mega-fan of Thomas Paine that he dug up Paine's body and had it shipped it to England, where he intended to build a proper memorial.

PAINE'S LEGACY FOR THE NATION

Paine's writings inspired presidents Andrew Jackson, Abraham Lincoln, and Ronald Reagan. During World War II, President Franklin Roosevelt used Paine's words to lift spirits of Americans in a radio address: "These are times that try men's souls … tyranny, like hell, is not easily conquered."

While Thomas Edison appreciated Paine as an inventor, he also helped him regain recognition for his role in the founding of America. In 1925, he wrote, "Tom Paine has almost no influence on present-day thinking in the United States because he is unknown to the average citizen … He was the equal of Washington in making American liberty possible."

Today, there are several statues worldwide dedicated to the life and historical significance of Thomas Paine. As Andrew Jackson said, though, "Thomas Paine needs no monument made by hands … *The Rights of Man* will be more enduring than all the piles of marble and granite that man can erect."

This statue of Paine in Thetford, England, depicts the author grasping a copy of his *Rights of Man* and wielding a quill, representing the enduring power of the written word.

GLOSSARY

aristocrat A privileged member of the elite or ruling class. Traditionally, the aristocracy holds a greater share of power, wealth, and political influence.

atheism A lack of belief in God or gods.

burlesque A comic exaggeration; a mockery.

colonies Settlements formed by people who have left their native country that are still connected with the parent nation.

corset A tightly fitting woman's undergarment that shapes a figure, extending from just beneath the chest to the hips.

effigy A model or crude representation of a person.

excise A tax charged on the sale of a certain good.

guillotine A machine with a heavy blade, designed for beheading people during the French Revolution.

hereditary Passed on from parents to their children or descendants.

incite To inspire an individual or group to take action; provoke.

morale A spirit of optimism in a person or group.

Parliament A law-making government body.

privilege A benefit or right enjoyed by a person or group beyond the advantages of most.

radical Favoring or pushing for drastic or extreme political, economic, or social reform.

representation Speaking or acting on the behalf of another or others.

republic A government in which power is held by the people and elected representatives.

sedition Action that incites people to rebel against the authority of the ruling government.

turmoil A state of extreme agitation or confusion.

typhoid fever A serious disease that often spreads by dirty food or water.

tyranny Cruel and oppressive government.

workhouse A place where the very poor in England once worked in exchange for food and shelter.

FOR MORE INFORMATION

American Civil Liberties Union

125 Broad Street, 18th Floor

New York, NY 10004

(212) 549-2500

Website: https://www.aclu.org/

Facebook: @aclu.nationwide

Twitter: @ACLU

The ACLU works to defend and preserve the individual rights and liberties guaranteed by the Constitution and the laws of the United States—a cause the corresponds to the beliefs of Thomas Paine.

Canadian Civil Liberties Association

90 Eglinton Avenue East, Suite 900

Toronto, ON M4P 1A6

Canada

(416) 363-0321

Website: https://ccla.org

Twitter: @cancivlib

Facebook: @cancivlib

The kinds of rights that Paine fought for are often referred to as civil liberties. This group, founded in 1964, is dedicated to fighting for civil liberties in Canada.

Thomas Paine Cottage Museum

20 Sicard Avenue

New Rochelle, NY 10804

(914) 633-1776

Website: http://www.thomaspainecottage.org

This museum is the last home that Paine owned in the United States. Visitors can learn about Paine, as well as life in early nineteenth-century New Rochelle.

Thomas Paine National Historical Association

983 North Avenue

New Rochelle, NY 10804

Website: http://www.thomaspaine.org

Email: tpnhamail@gmail.com

An organization dedicated to educating the world about the life, times, and works of Thomas Paine.

Thomas Paine Society

99 South Raymond Avenue, Suite B001

Pasadena, CA 91105

Website: http://www.thomaspainesociety.org

A nonprofit committed to educating the public about the life and works of Thomas Paine. It has often held celebrations to honor Paine on his birthday, January 29.

WEBSITES

Because of the changing nature of Internet links, Rosen Publishing has developed an online list of websites related to the subject of this book. This site is updated regularly. Please use this link to access the list:

http://www.rosenlinks.com/CIVC/Paine

FOR FURTHER READING

Archer, Jules. *They Made a Revolution: The Sons and Daughters of the American Revolution*. New York, NY: Sky Pony Press, 2016.

Hesleden, Michael. *Benjamin Franklin: Writer, Inventor, and Diplomat* (Spotlight on American History). New York, NY: PowerKids Press, 2016.

Hitchens, Christopher. *Thomas Paine's Rights of Man: A Biography*. New York, NY: Grove Press, 2008.

Jeffery, Gary. *Thomas Paine Writes Common Sense* (Graphic Heroes of the American Revolution). New York, NY: Gareth Stevens Publishing, 2011.

Kule, Elaine A. *12 Authors Who Changed the World* (Change Makers). North Mankato, MN: Peterson Publishing Company, 2016.

Nagelhout, Ryan. *Thomas Paine's Common Sense*. New York, NY: Gareth Stevens Publishing, 2013.

Paine, Thomas, with Harvey J. Kaye (forward). *Common Sense* (Complete and Unabridged). New York, NY: Clydesdale Press, 2017.

Perkins, Anne. *Trailblazers in Politics* (Original Thinkers). New York, NY: Rosen Publishing, 2015.

Rickman, Thomas Clio. *Life and Writings of Thomas Paine*. London, UK: Forgotten Books, 2016.

Waxman, Laura Hamilton. *Uncommon Revolutionary: A Story About Thomas Paine*. Minneapolis, MN: Lerner Publishing Group, 2003.

BIBLIOGRAPHY

Belchem, John. "Thomas Paine: Citizen of the World" BBC. Retrieved May 11, 2017. http://www.bbc.co.uk/history/british/empire_seapower/paine_01.shtml.

Bio.com. "Thomas Paine Biography." Retrieved March 6, 2017. http://www.biography.com/people/thomas-paine-9431951.

Collins, Paul. *The Trouble with Tom: The Strange Afterlife and Times of Thomas Paine*. New York, NY: Bloomsbury Publishing, 2005.

Gray, Edward. *Tom Paine's Iron Bridge: Building a United States*. New York, NY: W.W. Norton & Company, 2016.

The History Guide. "Thomas Paine, 1737–1809." Retrieved March 6, 2017. http://www.historyguide.org/intellect/paine.html.

Marrin, Albert. *Thomas Paine: Crusader for Liberty*. New York, NY: Alfred A. Knopf, 2014.

Smith, George Ford. "Thomas Paine, Liberty's Hated Torchbearer." June 8, 2010. https://mises.org/library/thomas-paine-libertys-hated-torchbearer.

USHistory.org. "Thomas Paine." Retrieved March 6, 2017. http://www.ushistory.org/paine.

Wilson, Jerome, and William F. Ricketson. *Thomas Paine*. Boston, MA: Twayne Publishers, 1989.

INDEX

Published in 2020 by The Rosen Publishing Group, Inc.
29 East 21st Street, New York, NY 10010

First Edition

Library of Congress Cataloging-in-Publication Data

Names: Uhl, Xina M., author.
Title: Juan Rodríguez Cabrillo : explorer of the American West Coast / Xina M. Uhl.
Description: First edition. | New York : Rosen Central, 2020 | Series: Our voices: Spanish and Latino figures of American history | Includes bibliographical references and index. | Audience: Grades 5–8.
Identifiers: LCCN 2018007104 | ISBN 9781508184904 (library bound) | ISBN 9781508184898 (pbk.)
Subjects: LCSH: Cabrillo, Juan Rodríguez, –1543—Juvenile literature. | Explorers—America—Biography—Juvenile literature. | Explorers—Spain—Biography—Juvenile literature. | America—Discovery and exploration—Spanish—Juvenile literature.
Classification: LCC E125.C12 U35 2019 | DDC 910.92 [B]—dc23
LC record available at https://lccn.loc.gov/2018007104

Manufactured in the United States of America

On the cover: Juan Rodríguez Cabrillo comes ashore on the California coast during his expedition of 1542. The log books of his journey state that the coastline was densely populated with native people.

CONTENTS

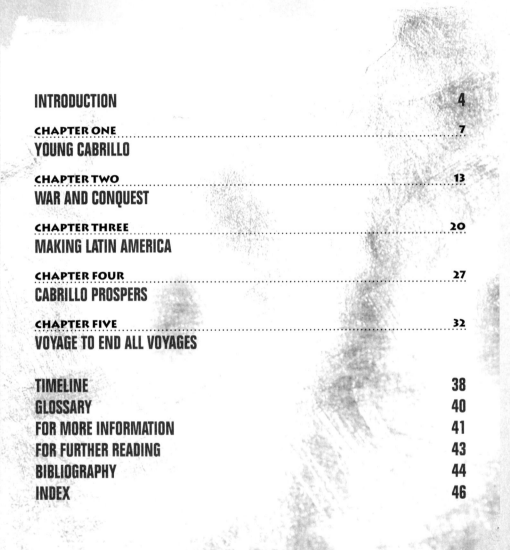

INTRODUCTION

Sixteenth-century Spanish conquistador Juan Rodríguez Cabrillo was many things. He was well known to fellow conquistadors who sailed from Spain to conquer and establish settlements in the New World—New Spain—in the Americas. In that role, he was very much a man of his time, and as such he participated in some of the most glorious—and horrifying—battles of the age alongside Hernán Cortés and other conquistadors. He became one of the founders of Guatemala and was a rich, powerful man with a sprawling estate there. He also became a skilled, sought-after shipbuilder. In 1541 a powerful earthquake took place while he was away from his home, in the capital city of Guatemala, Santiago. The bare, devastating account he wrote of the destroyed city was the first piece of journalism written in the New World.

In 1542 he took center stage in history when he became a ship's commander. He led an expedition north up the Pacific coast. There he became the first European to explore the west coast of North America. He provided the first written account of human activity on the West Coast in 1543. Though he died while the expedition was still traveling, his accomplishment echoed through the ages.

Despite his importance to what later became California, many details of his life are unknown or must be pieced together from records of his friends and commanders. Though he was a literate man, he was but one of several conquistadors named Juan Rodríguez. He did not take the name Cabrillo until

Explorer of
California
1542

29
USA

Juan Rodríguez
CABRILLO

The US Post Office issued a 29-cent commemorative stamp of Juan Rodríguez Cabrillo on September 28, 1992, 450 years to the day since he landed at San Diego Harbor.

1536. In between times he honed his skills as a seaman and a crossbow commander and fought alongside his fellow Spanish conquistadors in unknown lands, outnumbered and unable to escape. Fate favored Cabrillo and the Spanish—and devastated the Native Americans, who had no immunity to the diseases the Spanish brought and little defense against their superior weapons.

Though he participated in Hernán Cortés's conquest of the Aztec during his assault on New Spain, he found few riches at first. It was only after he joined a band of soldiers traveling even deeper into the heart of an unknown land that he became one of Guatemala's founders. His efforts as an estate owner, miner, and merchant added to his shipbuilding expertise—and led to the great wealth he had desired for so long. They were not to tell the end of his tale, however.

That came along with his greatest glory. As a conquistador, he discovered and claimed California for Spain, cementing his legacy as one of the most important Latino heroes in American history. Perhaps the Cabrillo National Monument Foundation sums up his legacy best when they say in an official account of his voyage: "Juan Rodríguez Cabrillo symbolizes the curiosity that drives us all to search for answers to the unknown, and the courage to risk everything for what we believe in."

CHAPTER ONE

YOUNG CABRILLO

Almost nothing is known of Cabrillo's childhood, except that he was born around 1498. For several hundred years, historians claimed that Cabrillo came from Portugal. Since then, though, many American historians became convinced that he came from Spain instead. Several villages in Portugal claim he was born there, though their proof remains elusive. However, at the time of Cabrillo's life, Portuguese pilots, or helmsmen, were famous for their skills. The matter remains up for debate, however.

As a youth, Cabrillo was known as Juan Rodríguez. He would not take the name Cabrillo for many years still. He grew up in an age begun by an explorer named Christopher Columbus, who set sail for Spain in search of new trade routes to India and Asia. Europeans wanted such a route because by the time goods came to Europe from the east, a network of merchants and brokers had driven up the prices. Europeans believed that if they could cut out the middlemen and trade directly with the east, they would keep more money for themselves. However, they did not know how to sail there.

THE LANDING OF COLUMBUS OCT. 11TH 1492.

Christopher Columbus is a controversial figure. A product of a violent era, he captured Native Americans as slaves. As governor of the Dominican Republic, he put down native revolts with much bloodshed.

A NEW WORLD

Columbus changed all that in 1492 when he arrived in the West Indies. Convinced that he had discovered a new route to India, he called the inhabitants Indians. What Columbus did not know was that he had found a way to lands that Europeans did not know existed. Europeans called these lands the New World, later known as the Americas. In the years following Columbus's voyages, other explorers came to conquer these lands.

CUBA'S CONQUEST

On his famed journey of discovery, Christopher Columbus landed on the island of Cuba on October 28, 1492. It was not until 1511, however, that a Spaniard named Diego Velázquez de Cuéllar joined Hernán Cortés to conquer Cuba. Over a four-year period Velázquez founded several settlements, one of which was Havana, also called La Habana. Another settlement was Baracoa on the northeastern coast. Velázquez settled it with three hundred Spaniards and their African slaves.

In 1514 Velázquez became Cuba's governor. He worked to attract colonists to the island, a difficult task at first because of a lack of gold deposits. Conquistadors were granted control over natives who lived in certain areas. The Spanish forced these natives to provide them with tribute.

The colony soon served as a staging ground for conquistadors to explore coastal areas along the Yucatán Peninsula and the Gulf of Mexico.

The Spanish conquistadors first settled in the Caribbean, on the islands of Hispaniola (today's Dominican Republic and Haiti), Cuba, and Puerto Rico. Although the Spanish had few soldiers compared to the millions of Native Americans that inhabited the New World, they had several important advantages. The guns, cannons, and armor they carried were superior to the natives'

Pánfilo de Narváez became one of Jamaica's first settlers as a young man. He later participated in military expeditions to Cuba, Mexico, and modern-day Florida.

arrows and spears. They made use of horses to carry supplies and during battle. Native Americans had never before seen horses and at first found them frightening. Finally—and most critically—the Native Americans had built up no resistance to the diseases carried by the Spanish. As a result, they died quickly from smallpox, cholera, and other fatal illnesses. Village upon village was wiped out. Up to 90 percent of Native Americans died in the 1500s.

The young Cabrillo traveled to Cuba in about 1510, when he was around twelve years old. There, Pánfilo de Narváez, commander of a company of archers who had helped conquer Cuba, saw to his education. That would have involved learning to write instructions and reports, reading ship logs and manifests, creating navigational charts, and making computations based on the stars.

THE COMING OF CORTÉS

The Spanish spread quickly from the Caribbean, exploring the coastal waters. They heard stories of grand cities of gold and fierce natives who defended them. Hernán Cortés, who owned land in Cuba, believed he could push through the Native Americans who defended these cities and take over the land for

Spain. Diego Velázquez, Cuba's first governor, appointed Cortés to lead an expedition to conquer Mexico. Velázquez soon came to regret that decision and changed Cortés's orders. Cortés ignored the new order. On February 18, 1519, Cortés sailed from Cuba with several hundred Spaniards and about three thousand natives in order to conquer the Mexican mainland.

DOÑA MARINA

Malinche was a Native American princess born in Mexico. When Cortés came to Tabasco, Mexico, the Tabascan natives gave him a peace offering: female slaves. One of these slaves, named Malinche, became Cortés's guide, interpreter, and mistress. She eventually bore him a son, whom they named Martín. Without her knowledge and assistance, he would not have succeeded in conquering Mexico.

Malinche has been known by various names throughout history. The Spanish called her La Lengua and Doña Marina while native languages refer to her as Malintzin or Malina.

Malinche converted to Christianity, and it was at this time that she changed her name to Doña Marina. She married one of Cortés's soldiers, Juan de Jaramillo. Together, they sailed to Spain, where the Spanish court welcomed her with open arms.

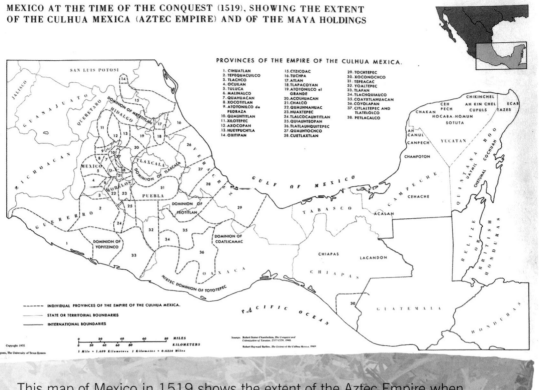

MEXICO AT THE TIME OF THE CONQUEST (1519), SHOWING THE EXTENT OF THE CULHUA MEXICA (AZTEC EMPIRE) AND OF THE MAYA HOLDINGS

This map of Mexico in 1519 shows the extent of the Aztec Empire when Cortés came. Because he left from Cuba, he approached Mexico from the Gulf of Mexico.

He and his men landed at Tabasco, Mexico, on the northern coastline. There he found an interpreter named Malinche, who served as an invaluable intercessor with the natives. She knew the Maya and Aztec languages, and she soon learned Spanish.

Cortés then performed a calculating, brilliant action to guarantee that his men would fight to the death for him. He burned the ships. Now he and his men were stranded in Mexico. They had no choice but to commit themselves to conquest or die trying.

CHAPTER TWO

WAR AND CONQUEST

Cortés's men marched through the Mexican interior, gathering Native American allies as they went. The Aztec Empire had made many enemies by sacrificing captives of their subject peoples. As a result of these brutal sacrifices, natives were eager to assist the Spanish. Over time, Cortés gathered more than two hundred thousand native allies.

Montezuma II, ruler of Mexico's Aztec empire, tried to keep Cortés from entering his large, beautiful capital, Tenochtitlán. The city sat on two islands in the middle of Lake Texcoco. Great causeways connected the city to the mainland. Cortés and his men, with a mere

The ruins shown here are all that remain of the seat of the Aztec Empire. The spot is called Templo Mayor, and today it is a museum.

THE GLORY OF TENOCHTITLÁN

In 1520 Cortés wrote a letter to Spain's ruler, Charles V. In it, he described Tenochtitlán:

> This great city is situated on a salt lake, and ... there are four entrances to the city formed by artificial causeways, two spears' length in width. The city is as large as Seville or Cordova; its principal streets are very wide and straight; some of these are half land and half water, and are navigated by canoes. Water flows from openings in the streets ... at these openings are bridges made of sturdy timber, and on many of them ten horses can go abreast.

> One of the city's squares contained more than sixty thousand people who came to the markets for jewels, gold, silver, birds such as parrots, small dogs (Chihuahuas), herbs, vegetables, maize, and more. The temples also amazed Cortés.

> Among these temples the greatest one is so large and beautiful that the human tongue cannot describe it. A wall encloses it where there is room enough for five hundred families ... There are fully forty towers, lofty and strong. The largest ... is higher than the tower of the principal tower of the church at Seville.

one thousand Native American allies, entered the city against Montezuma's wishes.

Despite this, Montezuma welcomed Cortés with great honor. But Cortés soon seized him in order to control the empire and insure that they convert to Christianity. Cortés pressured Montezuma to sign over his riches and his land to the Spanish. Cortés had become the ruler of Mexico.

A CHALLENGE TO CORTÉS

Cortés knew his position was not secure. He and his allies were holed up in Tenochtitlán, in a palace complex said to contain three hundred rooms, with the Aztec's imprisoned leader, Montezuma. Montezuma soon died. It is not clear whether this resulted from stones hurled at him by his people or at the hands of the Spanish.

This frieze located in the Rotunda of the US Capitol depicts Cortés and Montezuma at a Mexican temple. It was created by Constantino Brumidi, who lived from 1805 until 1880.

Sometime in 1520, Cortés received distressing news. Back in Cuba, Diego Velázquez had ordered Panfilo de Narváez to take a fleet of ships and nine hundred men to Mexico. Once there, Narváez would replace Cortés as leader of Mexico. Cortés had been charged with treason for ignoring Velázquez's orders not to go to Mexico and for declaring himself ruler of Mexico.

Cabrillo was one of the nine hundred men Velásquez sent after Cortés, under the command of Narváez. By this time, Cabrillo had grown into a skilled crossbowman and a man fit to lead the group of around nineteen archers. In later testimonies, Cabrillo's friends stated that by the time he went to Mexico he was also an experienced mariner. Narváez's force also included about eighty cavalry and seventy arquebusiers, who were soldiers armed with a kind of firearm. They landed near Vera Cruz at the end of April 1520. Cortés left Tenochtitlán to meet the force. Only his trusted lieutenant, Pedro de Alvarado, remained behind with 140 men.

Cortés snuck up on Narváez's men during a dark, rainy night. Though he had a small force compared to Narváez, he surprised them. Narváez's cannons had been sealed with wax to keep the gunpowder dry from the rain, so they could not be used. Cortés's men cut the saddle girths in the corral, keeping Narváez's cavalry from mounting up. Narváez's poorly trained men had been threatened with death if they did not fight. That, combined with Cortés's surprise attack, resulted in a short battle that Cortés won. Most of Narváez's soldiers—including Cabrillo—joined Cortés's force.

BACK IN TENOCHTITLÁN

With Cortés away from Tenochtitlán, Alvarado and his men found themselves threatened by the Aztecs. Alvarado sent word of the dire situation to Cortés, who hurried back to Tenochtitlán. Two weeks later, Cortés decided to abandon the city lest he and his men be outnumbered and overwhelmed by the Aztecs.

The Aztecs removed the city's causeway bridges and dug the water channels deeper and wider to make it easier to attack the Spanish. Cortés's force split into two groups and pushed forward, fighting across sections of the causeways. The group commanded by Alvarado, which included Cabrillo, had brought a portable wooden bridge with them so they could replace the ones the Aztecs had removed. Bit by bit, the Spanish fought forward, but the Aztec soldiers slaughtered many of them. Cortés's retreat

QUETZALCÓATL AND MONTEZUMA

An Aztec god known as the Feathered Serpent, Quetzalcóatl was one of the major gods of ancient Mexico. He started out as a god of vegetation closely associated with the god of rain. Over time he transformed into the god of the morning and evening star. By the time of Cortés, he had become the patron of priests, creator of calendars, and the symbol of death and resurrection.

Montezuma feared an uncertain fate as a result of predictions by Aztec astrologers. Many Aztecs feared the return of Quetzalcóatl as a bearded white man who would rule over the empire. When Cortés arrived he learned of this prophecy and used it to his advantage to gain power over the native peoples.

from the city lasted five days. Many of his men were killed, some of whom drowned because they refused to abandon the heavy gold treasure they had taken from the capital. But Cabrillo survived.

Now on the mainland, Cortés is said to have paused against a tree at the end of a causeway. There, he wept over the deaths of so many of his men.

In Tepaca, Cortés regrouped his army. He recruited more native allies and welcomed Spanish soldiers who had just arrived via ship. Cortés ordered thirteen brigantines to be built.

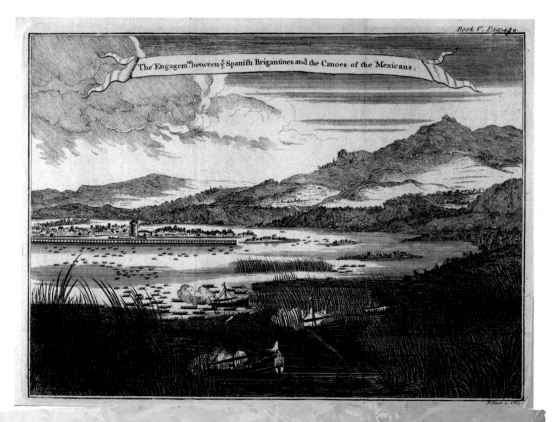

Today, Lake Texcoco has been largely drained. What remains of the lake sits 2.5 miles (4 kilometers) east of Mexico City, a shadow of its former size. This drawing shows Cortés's brigantines fighting Aztec canoes.

Cabrillo supervised the work, which was done by the natives. Part of his job involved gathering pitch and tallow to seal the ships' seams and protect the hulls from worms. The workers slashed and burned pine trees to extract the pitch.

In Europe, fat from cattle was made into tallow. With no cattle in Mexico, Cabrillo's men looked for another solution for the fat they needed. They found it in the bodies of the hostile Indians.

Once the brigantines were finished, they were then dismantled. Slaves carried them to Lake Texcoco and reassembled them.

Cortés gathered a huge force of about 150,000 native allies along with around a thousand Spaniards. Together, they launched an attack to retake Tenochtitlán. The brigantines fought against Aztec warriors in their canoes. When the Spanish regained control over the lake, they proceeded to fight on the causeways on foot and on horseback.

For eighty-five days the Aztecs fought fiercely, and most of the conquistadors that survived were wounded, including Cabrillo. The siege ended when the Spanish captured the Aztec's new leader, Montezuma's nephew.

CHAPTER THREE

MAKING LATIN AMERICA

When the ruler of Tenochtitlán surrendered to the Spanish on August 13, 1521, he unleashed chaos. The Spanish looted the city, and their native allies ran wild, slaughtering the Aztecs who had sacrificed their loved ones to bloodthirsty gods. Their anger was understandable, considering a Spanish account of a sacrifice by Fray Toribio de Benavente Motolinia: "The high priest who wielded the sacrificial knife struck the blows that smashed through the chest. He then thrust his hand into the cavity which he had opened to rip out the still beating heart. This he held high as an offering to the sun."

Some of the city's inhabitants tried to flee to the mainland in canoes, both during the daytime and also at night when they crashed into one another in their hurry. Many of the Aztecs had been suffering from smallpox spread to them by contact with the Spanish. Friar Bernadino de Sahagún described their plight: "The illness was so dreadful that no one could walk or move. The sick were so utterly helpless that they could only lie on the beds like corpses."

The conquistadors who sacked the city expected that they would grow rich with the spoils of the Aztecs, but such was not the case. One-fifth of the treasure was put aside for the king, and Cortés took his share as well. After the leftovers were divided among the remaining conquistadors, they found themselves

This vibrant Aztec shield is decorated with feathers and shows a water beast with a knife in its jaws. Likely a ceremonial piece, Montezuma may have given it to Cortés.

in possession of little more than glory. Disappointed and angry by the lack of treasure, Cortés pacified them by promising further expeditions into the Mexican interior, where they would undoubtedly gather more gold, silver, and precious jewels for themselves.

In years to come, Mexico City was established on the site of Tenochtitlán. The Cathedral of Mexico City stands on the very site where the temple pyramid complex stood.

THE SPANISH WAR MACHINE

At home in Spain, the men who later became conquistadors learned warfare. But the style of warfare that succeeded in Europe did not work in the New World. Instead, they adopted different tactics. They fought in small groups against large numbers of natives. Their superior weapons and soldiers mounted on horseback made them seem fearsome and gave them a psychological advantage. Small groups of these soldiers, wearing heavy metal armor, charged into the midst of native warriors again and again. The infantry followed them, armed with poleaxes, spears, swords, and shields.

For fighting at a distance, two weapons were best: the crossbow and the arquebus. The arquebus used gunpowder as a primitive musket. Most Native Americans had never experienced the devastating wounds—not to mention the smoke and deafening noise—of gunpowder weapons like the arquebus or cannons.

SUBDUING REBELLIONS AND FIGHTING FOR GOLD

Cabrillo appears to have profited enough from Tenochtitlán's fall that he acquired a horse, an expensive purchase at the time. He may have become a hidalgo, or an officer of importance. For his service, Cortés offered Cabrillo an encomienda.

An encomienda consisted of a right to demand labor or tribute from the natives of a certain area. This system entitled the Spanish to force Native Americans into virtual slavery, working under brutal conditions. Technically, the arrangement was supposed to benefit both parties. In exchange for the Native Americans' labor, the Spanish overlord, or encomendero, was required by the Spanish crown to protect them and teach them about Christianity. In practice, poor treatment combined with disease drastically reduced the number of natives.

Cabrillo refused Cortés's offer of an encomienda, but not from any objections to the treatment of natives. As a young man in his twenties, perhaps Cabrillo was not ready to settle down into such an estate. Or perhaps he figured he could enrich himself with further exploits. That turned out to be the case.

SPANISH SLAUGHTERS

Though no records testify to Cabrillo's participation in a brutal slaughter written about by the priest Bartolomé de Las Casas, he was almost certainly present during one grisly incident.

One day, after a long, tiring march, Narváez and three hundred of his men visited the Indian village of Caonao where the Indians welcomed them with a meal and fresh water. As they ate, the people examined the Spanish horses, which they had never seen before. As they pressed closer in curiosity, a soldier drew his sword. His

(continued on the next page)

(continued from the previous page)

fellow Spaniards leaped up and proceeded to hack at the bystanders with their swords. The slaughter included men, women, children, and even domestic animals. No one knows the number of natives killed, but it could have ranged between two and three thousand. The killings so disturbed Las Casas that he abandoned the expedition, telling Narváez, "You and your men can go to the devil."

The brutality displayed by the Spanish in the New World likely occurred in other incidents and inspired Las Casas to write an impassioned account to the king of Spain, hopeful that he would pass new laws to protect the Native Americans from further abuse.

The Spanish moved southward to subdue a rebellion of the Mixtec people. Cabrillo participated in a foray into Oaxaca under Francisco de Orozco in fall 1521. Little is known about his activities there. When Cabrillo joined an army commanded by Pedro de Alvarado, he commanded a squadron of crossbowmen. For the next ten years he and Alvarado worked to conquer Guatemala and suppress uprisings of the native people.

GUATEMALA

The conquest of Guatemala involved many obstacles. The first was the terrain, marked by tall mountains, volcanoes, dense jungles, plummeting ravines, cold rivers, and humid swamps. The native peoples were the second obstacle. Called the Quichés and Tzutuhils, they had descended from the ancient Maya people, the builders of vast cities, astronomical observatories, and sophisticated calendars. By the time the Spanish arrived many of the cities had fallen into ruins. Cabrillo was among Alvarado's men who fought several bloody battles against them before defeating sixteen thousand Tzutuhils in spring 1524. In April 1524, the group attacked Utatlán, the capital city of the Quichés. The city had been ruled by the same dynasty for twenty generations. Historian Hubert Howe Bancroft described the palace's marvels:

> It was built of hewn stone of various colors, mosaic in appearance, and its colossal dimensions, and elegant and stately architectural form, excited mingled awe and admiration … Next lay the residence of the unmarried princes, and beyond this the palace proper, containing besides the apartments of the monarch the council-chamber, with the gorgeous throne canopied with costly tapestry of feather work of rare designs and wrought with cunning skill; also the royal treasury, the hall of justice, and the armory.

This eighteenth-century color engraving shows Pedro de Alvarado's forces battling the native Utatlán people in 1524.

Three separate suites of rooms, for morning, afternoon, and night, were each day occupied by the monarch, and all these more private apartments looked out upon delightful gardens, with trees, and flowers, and fruits, and in their midst menageries and aviaries, with rare and curious collections. Beyond lay the separate palaces of the monarch's queens and concubines, with their baths, and gardens, and miniature lakes.

Alvarado destroyed Utatlán in a series of terrible battles. When the Quichés surrendered, Alvarado ordered the people branded and sold into slavery.

He proclaimed Guatemala's conquest complete in July 1524 when he established the capital in the former native village of Iximché. The new name of the city was Ciudad del Señor Santiago. Cabrillo signed the city's official register as a citizen and landowner on August 12. However, native uprisings continued and it took several years for the Spanish to march across Guatemala, Honduras, and El Salvador to the south before they truly triumphed.

CABRILLO PROSPERS

As an official citizen of Santiago in 1524, Cabrillo had special privileges. Only citizens could own their own land, as a reward for service they had done for the Spanish crown. He had earned a house lot, a farm lot of six hundred by fourteen hundred paces, and encomienda privileges. Also around 1524, Cabrillo likely took a native woman as a wife. Though her name is unknown, she lived with Cabrillo for many years. The couple had several children, at least three of which were daughters. These daughters later married conquistadors.

Cabrillo's wealth grew over the years, especially when in 1529 he and two companions, Diego Sánchez de Ortega and Sancho de Barahona, received permission to search for gold. In a town north of Santiago called Cobán, they found it. By now

No one knows for certain what Cabrillo looked like, but this engraved portrait is likely to be close to the reality.

Cabrillo had several encomiendas. The natives who gave service to him likely performed a number of tasks. One was raising chickens and farming for corn, beans, and chilies to eat and other crops to sell, such as cacao, from which chocolate is made. Though no record stands to testify to how Cabrillo treated the natives he controlled, other sources speak about the conditions faced by these native miners in other areas such as Cuba.

Las Casas wrote that he saw whole villages deprived of men, who had been sent to work in the fields. Starvation kept their wives from producing milk to nourish their babies. Thousands of native children may have died from such circumstances.

The natives also mined gold from the streams, which could be both difficult and fatal. Oviedo, who wrote for the Spanish crown, witnessed Native Americans panning for gold by standing in muddy mountain streams for days. A lack of food and rest caused them to grow sick and die. African slaves took their places. Though they fared better than the natives, they also suffered from disease, overwork, and malnutrition.

CABRILLO'S HOUSEHOLD

As Cabrillo's fortunes increased, so did his responsibilities. He cared for the members of his extended household as Spanish law dictated. This included more than just his family. He also supported distant relatives, friends, nobles down on their luck, military aides, maiden women, orphans or children of other conquistadors, servants, and household slaves.

In 1532, Cabrillo returned to Spain. There, he married his friend Diego's sister, Beatriz Sánchez de Ortega, in a prearranged union, which was customary at the time. The couple sailed to Guatemala in 1533 and over time had at least two sons, one named Juan

Rodríguez Cabrillo like his father and the other named after his friend and in-law, Diego Sánchez de Ortega.

By the mid-1530s, Cabrillo was one of Santiago's leading citizens. The first official records with his name as Juan Rodríguez Cabrillo appear in July 1536, when Alvarado awarded him the pueblos of Teota and Cotela as reward for his help in putting down an uprising in Honduras. No one knows why he took the name Cabrillo. It may have been a nickname or a means of honoring the town he came from.

Along with running his estate and managing his mines, he also gained wealth as a merchant and shipbuilder. In 1536 Pedro de Alvarado, Guatemala's governor, decided to build a fleet of ships to explore the Pacific. He commissioned Cabrillo to manage the project, located near the fishing village of Iztapa. Cabrillo himself covered the cost of one of these ships, a 200-ton (181-metric ton) galleon with two decks called the *San Salvador*. By 1540, Cabrillo had overseen construction of seven or eight vessels that Alvarado wanted to trade between Central America and the Spice Islands.

THE EVILS OF SHIPBUILDING

The village of Iztapa near Alvarado's shipyard was a small, miserable place. To make life better for the men, Cabrillo and another Spanish official, Alvara de Paz, ordered press-gangs to round up dozens of Native American

(continued on the next page)

(continued from the previous page)

girls and women to serve as cooks, launderers, and bed companions. The bishop, Marroquín, protested the women's treatment and asked for the king of Spain to intervene. But by the time his letter arrived the fleet was nearly complete.

Native American men also experienced poor treatment. The priest Bartolomé de Las Casas detailed the brutality they suffered:

> From the north to the south sea a hundred and thirty leagues the Indians carried anchors … which cut furrows into the shoulders and loins of some of them. And he [Alvarado] carried in the same way much artillery on the shoulders of these sad, naked people; and I saw many loaded with artillery on those anguished roads.

This letter was written by Friar Bartolomé de Las Casas, who documented abuses of the native peoples and was the first person appointed Protector of the Indians.

While Cabrillo attended to business away from Guatemala, an earthquake took place on September 11, 1541, in the middle of the night. A flood of water, mud, and rocks destroyed most of the houses. Alvarado's palace and almost everyone living there, including his wife, were killed. Hundreds of people died throughout the city, including six hundred Native Americans. Cabrillo returned home shortly thereafter. He wrote a report to the king about the destruction but was lucky enough not to lose his family or property in the temblor. His account of the earthquake was printed in a pamphlet in 1541 and distributed in Mexico. This made it the first piece of journalism in the New World.

In 1539, Alvarado died during an Indian uprising. Alvarado's partner in the venture, the viceroy of New Spain, Antonio de Mendoza, appointed Cabrillo to lead one of two expeditions to explore the Pacific. Following the earthquake, Cabrillo returned to the port at Navidad and made ready to leave on the voyage of his life.

CHAPTER FIVE

VOYAGE TO END ALL VOYAGES

On June 27, 1542, Juan Rodríguez Cabrillo captained an expedition that sailed out of the Mexican port of Navidad. The flagship was the *San Salvador*. A frigate (a kind of sailing ship for war) named the *Victoria* also went along. Bartolomé Ferrelo served as the chief pilot. In addition to the trade goals favored by Mendoza and Cortés, Cabrillo also sought the fabled seven rich cities known as Cibola that some believed were near the Pacific coast beyond New Spain. Finally, he looked for a route to connect the Pacific Ocean to the Atlantic Ocean.

The ships carried few provisions, and the crew consisted mainly of conscripts and natives with little sailing experience.

This painting, which depicts Cabrillo and his men landing at Las Canoas in 1542, hangs on a wall in the Santa Barbara, California, County courthouse.

Cabrillo and his men probably planned to resupply by trading with the Native Americans on land.

The ship inched up the coastline. On August 21, the expedition discovered Port San Quentín. The next day they went ashore and Cabrillo took formal possession of the country in the name of the viceroy and king. The natives they met communicated that other Spaniards with beards, dogs, and weapons were traveling five days inland. These Spaniards were probably from Francisco Coronado's expedition, which also had been sent forth

AN AMAZON ISLAND

Hernán Cortés believed that an expedition into unfamiliar waters might have an unusual find. He wrote to a relative in 1524 about rumors that claimed there were "many provinces thickly inhabited by people and containing, it is believed, great riches, and that in these parts of it there is one which is inhabited by women, with no men, who procreate in the way which the ancient histories ascribe to the Amazons and because by learning the truth regarding this and whatever else there is on said coast, God our Lord and their Majesties will be greatly served."

Cabrillo's expedition never ended up finding such a place, nor did they locate the mythical cities of Cibola or a strait that connected the Pacific and Atlantic Oceans. The reason for these failures was simple. None of these places existed.

after the cities of Cibola. Coronado traveled through eastern Arizona before turning east. Eventually, he ended up in Kansas before he turned back to Mexico, having failed in his mission.

CALIFORNIA!

One hundred and three days into Cabrillo's expedition, the expedition came into San Diego bay. According to the Juan Rodríguez Cabrillo National Monument, he probably came ashore near Ballast Point. There, he claimed the land for Spain, as he would do repeatedly. He called the bay San Miguel. When the explorer Sebastian Vizcaino arrived sixty years later, he changed the name to San Diego.

The expedition continued north to land in Santa Monica Bay. Cabrillo called the place Bahía de los Fumos ("Bay of Smokes") because of the smoke from many Native American fires. They sailed on northward to San Buenaventura. In the Channel Islands just off the coast they lingered for the next two months, sailing along the coast, exploring the area, and making contact with the local Chumash people. During this time, Cabrillo fell and broke his arm. Some historians say he may have fallen on the rocky shore. Others believe his broken arm came as a result of a brief skirmish with the natives.

The expedition headed northward again by mid-November and made it to near Point Reyes north of San Francisco. They did not sail near the coast, fearing shipwreck. Because of this, they sailed past San Francisco Bay, which was probably obscured by fog. Several explorers missed it entirely, so it remained undiscovered until 1769.

Along the way they contacted a number of native peoples and referred to certain areas as "densely populated." In order to prove their goodwill they captured several natives, gave them gifts, and let them go. These actions helped them to gain the natives' trust.

A DANGEROUS WINTER

Strong winds and storms compelled them to head southward for shelter at Point Concepción. They sailed again to San Miguel Island in the Channel Islands. There they remained for the winter, from November 23 to January 19. Nearly continual storms battered the ocean during this time.

On January 3, 1543, Cabrillo died as a result of complications from his broken arm. The spot of his burial remains unknown, although a stone slab found on Santa Rosa Island in 1901 may have marked it.

Command fell to Ferrelo, who moved the expedition to Santa Rosa Island. Ferrelo set sail northward again on February 18. After passing the northern-most point that Cabrillo had reached, they continued on before reaching a latitude around Rogue River, Oregon. Heading southward again, a heavy rainstorm caused the two ships to separate; they would be reunited three weeks later.

This aerial photo shows Santa Rosa Island, near the California coast. A dry, rugged island, it has only six native plant species and three native mammals.

In early March, the crew experienced a great deal of difficulty as they sailed. The *Relation of the Voyage of Juan Rodriguez Cabrillo, 1542–1543,* describes the vicious weather: "The wind shifted to the northwest and to the north-northwest with great fury, forcing them to scud to the southeast and east-southeast until Saturday the 3rd of March, with a sea so high that they became crazed, and if God and his blessed Mother had not miraculously saved them they could not have escaped. On Saturday at midday the wind calmed down and remained in the northwest, for which they gave heartfelt thanks to our Lord." The expedition sought brief haven on Santa Cruz Island. After the two ships reunited the journey home continued. They returned to Navidad on April 14, nine and a half months after they left.

BEYOND SILVER AND GOLD: CABRILLO'S DISCOVERIES

In the minds of the Spanish who sent Cabrillo's expedition up the Pacific coast, it was a failure. Cabrillo died, and they did not find gold or silver. They had not located a passage between the Pacific and Atlantic Oceans, because it did not exist. The cities of Cibola were a myth, a lesson that Coronado would also learn, to his dismay.

But Cabrillo's voyage provided the first written glimpse of the west coast of North America. It brought knowledge of the peoples, seas, landscape, and resources in the area, paving the way for other Spanish colonizers to expand their empire by settlement. These colonizers cemented Spain's claim over California. Cabrillo's route was not attempted again for sixty years.

Cabrillo was one of many Latino explorers whose bold efforts to plunge into a continent unknown to them left their mark on the Americas. Without their conquests the history of the West, Mexico, and South America would be very different. Spanish culture, language, and religion have merged with that of the native peoples to create a hybrid civilization.

California's population grew slower than other parts of New Spain, being so far north of Mexico City and the Spanish government. Mexican independence in 1821 ended Spain's hold on its North American empire. Massive population growth did not happen until the Gold Rush in 1848 brought a different kind of treasure seeker to the West. Soon California changed hands again, this time to the United States.

Today, Cabrillo is honored mostly by the names of schools, streets, and other public institutions in California. In 1913

This statue of Cabrillo appears at the Cabrillo National Monument. It is located on a rise that affords a nearly 360-degree view of San Diego and Mexico.

President Woodrow Wilson authorized the creation of the Cabrillo National Monument in San Diego, California. The monument was built in sight of Cabrillo's likely landing place. It includes a park with hiking trails, a lighthouse, tide pools, and historical exhibits.

TIMELINE

1492 Christopher Columbus arrives in the New World.

1498 Approximate birthdate of Juan Rodríguez Cabrillo.

1510 Approximate date Cabrillo leaves Spain for Cuba.

1511 Conquest of Cuba.

February 18, 1519 Hernán Cortés and a small army leave Cuba to conquer Mexico.

April 1520 Cabrillo goes to Mexico under Panfilo de Narváez's command. His force is defeated by Cortés, and Cabrillo joins Cortés's army.

August 13, 1521 Surrender and destruction of Tenochtitlán.

1520s–1530s Cabrillo joins his fellow Spanish conquistadors in conquering Guatemala and suppressing native uprisings.

Spring 1524 Cabrillo and Pedro de Alvarado conquer the Quichés and Tzutuhils and seize their capital.

July 1524 Alvarado declares Guatemala's conquest complete.

1532 Cabrillo sails to Spain and marries Beatriz Sánchez de Ortega.

1536 The first appearance of the name Cabrillo in official records. Before this he had been simply Juan Rodríguez. Cabrillo is commissioned to manage shipbuilding projects.

1540 Cabrillo finishes building ships and is appointed commander of a voyage of exploration along the Pacific coast.

September 11, 1541 Terrible earthquake occurs in Santiago, Guatemala. Cabrillo writes a widely circulated account of the destruction.

June 27, 1542 Cabrillo's voyage of discovery begins.

January 3, 1543 Cabrillo dies as a result of complications from a broken arm.

April 14, 1543 Cabrillo's expedition returns home.

GLOSSARY

arquebus A portable but heavy firearm usually fired using a tripod or other support.

artillery Large firearms like cannons.

brigantine A ship with two masts and square rigging.

cacao A tree that grows yellow seed pods that are dried and made into cocoa and chocolate.

causeway A raised road or path across water.

cholera A disease that involves severe diarrhea and vomiting.

conquistador A Spanish soldier involved in the sixteenth-century conquest of America.

encomienda A grant by the Spanish king allowing an American colonist to demand forced labor and tribute from an area's Native American inhabitants.

galleon A large sailing ship used by the Spanish from the fifteenth through the seventeenth centuries.

girth The band around a horse's body that keeps a saddle in place.

hidalgo A minor noble in Spain.

maize The Native American word for corn.

manifest A list of cargo or passengers on a ship.

mariner A sailor or ship navigator.

Maya A group of Native American people in the Yucatán Peninsula.

pitch Resin from pine trees used in the construction of sixteenth-century ships.

press-gang To cause a person to join military service against his will.

pueblo A village.

smallpox A disease caused by a virus that includes a fever and skin rash.

tallow Fat from cattle or sheep used in certain products, like lubricants.

FOR MORE INFORMATION

America in Class c/o National Humanities Center
7 TW Alexander Drive
PO Box 12256
Research Triangle Park, NC 27709
(919) 549-0661
Website: http://americainclass. org/primary-sources
Facebook: @NHC.EDUCATION
Twitter: @NHCEducation
This site collects a number of important primary sources across different time periods in American history. The exploration tab "American beginnings: the European presence in North America: 1492–1690" lists numerous documents and reading guides designed to make this time in history come alive through the eyes of the people who were there.

American Museum of Natural History
Central Park West at 79th Street
New York, NY 10024-5192
(212) 769-5100
Website: https://www.amnh .org/exhibitions /permanent-exhibitions /human-origins-and -cultural-halls/hall-of -mexico-and-central -america
Facebook: @naturalhistory
Twitter and Instagram: @amnh
The Hall of Mexico and Central America includes the 20-ton Aztec Stone of the Sun, gold objects, jeweled sculptures, and much more. Look at more than 1,400 artifacts online in the Virtual Hall.

Canadian Museum of History
100 Laurier Street
Gatineau, QC K1A 0M8
Canada
(800) 555-5621
Website: http://www .historymuseum.ca
Facebook, Twitter, and Instagram: @CanMusHistory
The museum features more than eighty exhibits on the history of the great explorers in Europe and Asia. Some are accessible online, while others are present in the museum on a rotating basis.

Library of Congress
101 Independence Ave SE
Washington, DC 20540
(202) 707-5000
Website: http://www.loc.gov
Facebook: @libraryofcongress
Twitter and Instagram:
    @librarycongress
The ongoing exhibition
    "Exploring the Early
    Americas" features more
    than three thousand rare
    maps, documents, artifacts,
    and paintings. Multiple
    collections reveal American
    history in art, documents,
    and artifacts from the
    exploration of the Americas.

Mariner's Museum
100 Museum Drive
Newport News, VA 23606
(800) 581- 7245
Website: http://exploration
    .marinersmuseum.org
Facebook, Twitter, and
    Instagram:
    @marinersmuseum
This museum provides
    extensive information on the
    explorers, ships, and tools
    from the Age of Discovery.

Metropolitan Museum of Art
1000 5th Avenue
New York, NY 10028
(212) 535-7710
Website: http://www
    .metmuseum.org/toah/hd
    /expl/hd_expl.htm
Facebook, Twitter, and
    Instagram: @metmuseum
Visitors will see original maps,
    essays, and art from the
    Age of Exploration.

Natural History Museum of Los Angeles County
900 Exposition Boulevard
Los Angeles, CA 90007
(213) 763-DINO
Website: https://nhm.org/site
Facebook, Twitter, and
    Instagram: @nhmla
The California History Hall
    includes an elaborate
    diorama that re-creates
    Juan Rodríguez Cabrillo's
    San Salvador and includes
    information on the crew and
    supplies based on records
    from the original ship log.

FOR FURTHER READING

Clarke, Catriona, Adam Larkum, Laura Parker, and Josephine Thompson. *Aztecs*. London, UK: Usborne, 2015.

Dawson, Patricia. *First Peoples of the Americas and the European Age of Exploration*. New York, NY: Cavendish Square Publishing, 2016.

Greek, Joe. *Hernán Cortés: Conquistador, Colonizer, and Destroyer of the Aztec Empire*. New York, NY: Rosen Publishing, 2017.

Haines, Serena. *Exploration of California*. Huntington Beach, CA: Teacher Created Materials, 2018.

Keller, Susanna. *Age of Exploration*. New York, NY: Britannica Educational, 2016.

Kenney, Karen Latchana. *Ancient Aztecs*. Minneapolis, MN: Abdo Publishing, 2015.

Loria, Laura. *La Malinche: Indigenous Translator for Hernán Cortés in Mexico*. New York, NY: Britannica Educational Publishing, 2018.

Mooney, Carla, and Tom Casteel. *Explorers of the New World: Discover the Golden Age of Exploration*. White River Junction, VT: Nomad Press, 2011.

Pletcher, Kenneth. *The Age of Exploration: From Christopher Columbus to Ferdinand Magellan*. New York, NY: Britannica Educational Publishing, 2014.

Shea, Therese. *The Land and Climate of Latin America*. New York, NY: Britannica Educational Publishing, 2018.

BIBLIOGRAPHY

American Journeys Collection: Wisconsin Historical Society Digital Library and Archives. "Relation of the Voyage of Juan Rodriguez Cabrillo 1542–1543." Document No. AJ-001. http://www.americanjourneys.org.

Conquistadors: Fall of the Aztecs. "The Last Stand: An Aztec Iliad." PBS. http://www.pbs.org/conquistadors/cortes/cortes_i00.html.

Jarus, Owen. "Tenochtitlán: History of Aztec Capital." Livescience, June 15, 2017. https://www.livescience.com/34660-tenochtitlan.html.

Kelsey, Harry. *Cabrillo.* San Marino, CA: Huntington Library, 1986.

Las Casas, Bartolomé de. *A Brief Account of the Destruction of the Indies Or, a faithful NARRATIVE OF THE Horrid and Unexampled Massacres, Butcheries, and all manner of Cruelties, that Hell and Malice could invent, committed by the Popish Spanish Party on the inhabitants of West-India, TOGETHER With the Devastations of several Kingdoms in America by Fire and Sword, for the space of Forty and Two Years, from the time of its first Discovery by them.* Project Gutenberg, 2007. http://www.gutenberg.org/cache/epub/20321/pg20321-images.html.

National Park Service. "*Juan Rodríguez Cabrillo.*" https://www.nps.gov/cabr/learn/historyculture/juan-Rodríguez-cabrillo.htm.

Nauman, James D, ed. *An Account of the Voyage of Juan Rodríguez Cabrillo.* San Diego, CA: Cabrillo National Monument Foundation, 1999.

Pourade, Richard F. *The Explorers.* San Diego, CA: Union-Tribune Publishing, 1960. https://www.sandiegohistory.org

/wp-content/uploads/migrated/books/pourade/explorers
/explorers.pdf.

Thatcher, Oliver J., ed. "Hernan Cortés: from Second Letter to
Charles V, 1520." Library of Original Sources. Milwaukee, WI:
University Research Extension Co., 1907. Vol. V: 9th to 16th
Centuries, pp. 317–326. https://sourcebooks.fordham.edu
/halsall/mod/1520cortes.asp.

INDEX

Published in 2020 by The Rosen Publishing Group, Inc.
29 East 21st Street
New York, NY 10010

First Edition

Produced for Rosen by Calcium Creative Ltd
Editors for Calcium: Sarah Eason and Tim Cooke
Designer: Paul Myerscough and Jessica Moon
Picture researcher: Rachel Blount

Photo credits: Cover: Shutterstock: Everett Historical; Inside: Library of Congress: John Herbert Evelyn Partington: p. 33; Shutterstock: Amanda Carden: p. 6; Everett Historical: pp. 34; KOSKA ill: pp. 3, 27; Marzolino: pp. 24–25; Petar Mulaj: p. 4; Jaroslav Sekeres: pp. 28–29; Tancha: p. 22; Tkachuk: p. 5; Faiz Zaki: p. 42; Wikimedia Commons: pp. 10, 13, 17, 26, 30, 38; Chistopher Brown: p. 18; John Collier: p. 19; Cristóvão de Morais: p. 11; Paul Delaroche: pp. 1, 14–15; Henry Howe: pp. 20–21; Internet Archive Book Images: p. 25br; Angela K. Kepler: p. 35; Frank E. Kleinschmidt: p. 36; Joseph Martin Kronheim: p. 8; George Washington Lambert: p. 32; Library of Congress: p. 39; Metropolitan Museum of Art: p. 7; Mostafameraji: pp. 12–13t; Nikolal Nevrev: p. 16; Samuel Augustus Perry: p. 23; Provincial Archives of Alberta: p. 37; Carole Raddato from Frankfurt. Germany: p. 9; Rowanda: p. 31; Richard Sigali: pp. 40–41; U.S. Navy Mass Communications Specialist 2nd Class Eric A. Pastor: p. 43.

Cataloging-in-Publication Data

Names: George, Enzo.
Title: Mysterious disappearances in history / Enzo George.
Description: New York : Rosen Central, 2020. | Series: The paranormal throughout history | Includes glossary and index.
Identifiers: ISBN 9781725346642 (pbk.) | ISBN 9781725346581 (library bound)
Subjects: LCSH: Disappearances (Parapsychology)—Juvenile literature.
Classification: LCC BF1389.D57 G47 2020 | DDC 001.94—dc23

Cover: In 1937 US pilot Amelia Earhart mysteriously disappeared during a flight over the Pacific Ocean.

CONTENTS

CHAPTER 1
THE LOST LEADERS

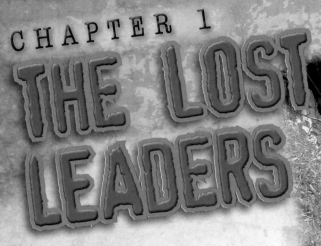

Throughout history, people have disappeared in mysterious circumstances. Some have set out on journeys, never to arrive at their destinations. Some are said to have been taken up to the heavens. Others have vanished with no explanation. They may have been murdered or carried on living under a new identity—or they may have been victims of the paranormal, a world some people believe lies beyond the world humans can observe using their senses.

This image depicts what it might look like if a person vanished into thin air. Is it possible that this has ever happened?

Disappearing Acts

In the past, people could "disappear" simply by moving a few miles from home. Without painted portraits or, later, photographs, even people such as kings and queens were only recognized by a few people. That made it easy for people to seem to disappear. Often, people probably did not disappear at all. It is just that there are no records of them.

The Queen Becomes King?

Nefertiti was the wife of the ancient Egyptian king Akhenaten. She had great power, because she ruled alongside her husband. After the 12th year of his reign, however, her name simply vanishes from the records. No one knows what became of her. She may have died, but if so, why was her death not recorded?

Records from tomb paintings show that Akhenaten took on another king at that time to rule with him. Some historians think this new "king" was actually Nefertiti. Others believe the new king played a part in having Nefertiti removed from power. She may have spent the rest of her life taking care of Akhenaten's children, who included a boy who would become Egypt's most famous ruler—Tutankhamun.

This famous statue of Nefertiti shows the beautiful queen as she may have looked in ancient times.

Hidden Hunter

Some science fiction authors, including the British writer Philip E. High, have played with the idea that an early form of life called protoplasm, a jelly-like mass, lives within Earth. Some say that, once or twice a century, it awakes to feed on people, whom it dissolves, leaving pools of water. Could this be an explanation for mysterious disappearances throughout history?

THE FOUNDER OF ROME

According to legend, the city of Rome was founded by the twin brothers Romulus and Remus, sons of the god Mars. The brothers argued, however, and Romulus killed Remus. Romulus became the first ruler of the city, which was named in his honor. Rome grew to become wealthy and powerful.

Into Thin Air

One day, according to the Roman historian Livy, Romulus was inspecting troops when a storm broke out. A large cloud came down from the sky and hid Romulus from view. Livy said, "From that moment on, he was never spotted again anywhere in the world." Another writer, Plutarch, said Romulus disappeared during a solar eclipse, when the moon blocks the light of the sun. He said that Earth plunged into darkness, and a terrible storm began. When daylight returned, Romulus had vanished.

Some Romans claimed Romulus had been murdered by the senators. These men made up Rome's senior council, and they wanted to be free of Romulus's rule. In the darkness, people said, the senators killed Romulus and cut his body into pieces that they then hid under their robes.

A solar eclipse can last for several hours, although they more often last for less than 10 minutes.

A God on Earth?

Another version of the story was provided by a noble who said he met Romulus after his disappearance. He said the king was wearing armor that flashed so brightly it hurt the eyes. The figure of Romulus explained that he was really the god Quirinus, who had been sent to live on Earth to help the Romans create a great civilization. Now his task was completed, he was returning to the gods. The Romans worshipped the god Quirinus for more than 1,000 years, before the city and its empire fell in 476 CE.

This engraving shows Romulus rising to heaven in a cloud and being welcomed as a god.

A Slave Leader

Spartacus was trained as a gladiator, or professional fighter, in ancient Rome. In 73 BCE, he led an army of gladiators and slaves in a rebellion against the rulers of Rome. In 71 BCE, Spartacus fought the Roman army at Senerchia in Italy. Defeat was almost certain, so he killed his own horse to make sure he would not be able to flee. He probably died on the battlefield—but there was no record of his death. Some people claim that the rebel escaped and lived out the rest of his life peacefully, in disguise.

WARRIOR QUEEN

The Romans landed in Britain in 55 BCE. They soon left, but returned in 43 CE, under Emperor Claudius. Some British tribes welcomed the Romans, because their arrival encouraged trade. Others decided to resist the invaders. They included the Iceni, who lived in southeast England under the rule of King Prasutagus.

Boudica and her army captured three cities in Roman Britain, including London.

Roman Revolt

After Prasutagus died in 60 CE, the Romans began to seize Iceni land. The king's wife Boudica led the Iceni in a full-scale revolt against the Romans. While the Roman army was on the other side of the country, she seized most of southeast England. Other tribes joined the Iceni, and by the time Boudica marched on the city of Londinium (London), she led 100,000 warriors. In all, the queen's armies killed up to 80,000 Roman and British civilians.

Boudica finally fought the Romans in the Battle of Watling Street. No one knows the location of the battle, but it was on a well-used Roman road. The queen's forces outnumbered the Romans, but the Romans were better armed and trapped the British where they could kill them easily.

8

The Fate of the Queen

Roman writers differ about what happened to Boudica. Some say she died in the defeat and was given a warrior's funeral. Others say that Queen Boudica died afer taking poison when her daughters were killed in the battle.

In the twentieth century, a new story circulated, claiming that the battle took place near London and that Boudica is buried under a platform at what is now King's Cross Station. In the past, some people believed that she was buried at Stonehenge, an ancient monument in southern England. However, experts now know that Stonehenge was built far earlier than Roman times.

Roman legionaries, or soldiers, were the most feared and best-trained warriors in ancient Europe.

The Lost Legion

The mystery of what happened to one of Rome's legions, or units of soldiers, has lasted for nearly 2,000 years. As far as historians can tell, the whole Legio XI, or Ninth Legion, of between 4,000 and 5,000 men simply disappeared. In 43 CE, the Ninth Legion joined the Roman conquest of Britain. It headed north to invade Caledonia (Scotland) in 82–83, then vanished from the records. Modern experts guess that the legion was wiped out by the Caledonians, who made a surprise attack on the Romans.

CHAPTER 2
HIDDEN HEROES

The Middle Ages, which lasted from about 500 to 1500, were a time when soldiers, merchants, sailors, and other adventurers might travel long distances without being able to send home any news. Marco Polo, the Venetian merchant, spent 24 years traveling in Asia, for example, before finally making it home.

When he got there, people were shocked to see him because they had assumed he must be dead. It was during the Middle Ages that legends started to grow up around missing heroes, saying that one day they would return when their people were in greatest need.

The Missing King

Some disappearances were the subject of great debate. This was particularly true of rulers, such as King Sebastian of Portugal, who led his army into Morocco in 1578 to fight the region's Muslim rulers. The Portuguese were badly defeated and Sebastian was thought to have been killed. Two years later, the throne of Portugal passed to the Spanish ruler, King Philip II.

In this illustration, Marco Polo arrives at an Asian city during his travels between 1271 and 1295. His was one story with a happy ending, when he finally made it home!

10

The Four Sebastians

Philip claimed to have buried Sebastian, but many Portuguese did not believe him. A movement emerged known as Sebastianism. Its followers said that the king had survived and was ready to return at any moment to remove Philip and reclaim his rightful throne. Over the next 60 years, four men claimed to be the returning king. They were all put on trial by King Philip, found guilty of being imposters, and then killed.

The death or disappearance of Sebastian was seen as the start of a long decline in Portugal's national fortunes.

Waiting to Help

Sebastian was said to be waiting to come to Portugal's rescue in its time of greatest need. A similar story was told about a Welsh king named Owain Glyndwr, who led a revolt against Wales' English rulers. Glyndwr vanished from history in about 1412, after a raid on English forces. Some rumors said he was dead, but the English offered a huge reward for his capture. When King Henry V came to the throne the following year, he offered Glyndwr a royal pardon if he gave himself up—but the Welshman never reappeared. One story said he died quietly in 1415; others said that he was another national hero waiting to come to the aid of his countrymen when needed.

11

THE HIDDEN IMAN

The Islamic religion was founded by the Prophet Muhammad in Saudi Arabia in 610 CE. Within just a few decades, the new faith had spread through much of the Middle East. However, it also became divided into hostile groups known as Shias and Sunnis.

The Faith Splits

Over the next centuries, the Shia form of Islam also split into different branches. The largest, which is today followed by 85 percent of Shias, is called Twelver. Twelvers believe Allah, or God, chose a series of 12 spiritual leaders, known as the Twelve Imams, to follow the first Shia imam, Ali. Their task was to interpret the words of Muhammad to show Muslims how to live on Earth.

The 12th imam, Muhammad al-Mahdi, became imam when he was five. Few people ever saw him, and he had contact with his followers only through his trusted deputies. In 878, he sent his followers a letter saying that he would disappear from Earth—and was never seen again. He then became known as the Hidden Iman.

The Hidden Imam is said to have appeared to order the building of the Jamkaran Mosque in Qom in Iran.

The Sleeping Hero

The Hidden Imam is an example of what people who study myths and legends call a sleeping hero. The phrase describes a leader who has vanished from Earth but who is said to be waiting to return. Other examples of sleeping heroes include King Arthur, who is said to sleep in a cave awaiting the call to help Great Britain, and the twelfth-century German King Charlemagne. He is said to sleep with his knights in a cave beneath a mountain, waiting to restore Germany to greatness. His red beard is said to be so long that it has grown through the table where he sleeps!

Return to Earth

Twelvers believe Muhammad al-Mahdi still lives, but has been hidden by Allah in a process called occultation. This was said to be both in order to protect the imam and to test the faith of the Shias. The Hidden Imam is said to walk Earth in disguise, sometimes making himself known.

Twelvers believe the Hidden Imam will return to Earth, alongside Jesus Christ, in a form known as the Mahdi. They say he will reappear at Mecca, the Islamic holy city, on a Friday. He will lead the Shias in warfare against the Sunnis and afterward will bring peace and justice to the world.

King Arthur was said to have been taken to a mysterious place named the Isle of Avalon at the end of his life.

13

THE PRINCES IN THE TOWER

One of the most dangerous times for a medieval ruler was when he claimed his throne. There were often people ready to seize power if the rightful heir disappeared—or could be made to disappear. Sometimes, these challenges came from close to home.

The Lost Boys

When English King Edward IV died in 1483, the throne passed to his elder son, who became King Edward V. Edward was just 12 years old, so he and his younger brother, Richard, Duke of York, were placed in the care of their uncle, Richard, Duke of Gloucester. The duke was meant to govern the country until Edward was old enough to take the throne himself.

The Duke of Gloucester sent the boys to live in the Tower of London, where monarchs usually waited to be crowned. However, the duke first delayed Edward's coronation, and then canceled it. Instead, he had himself proclaimed King Richard III. He was crowned in July 1483.

Soon afterward, the two young princes disappeared. People guessed they had been killed on Richard's orders, so their supporters could not question Richard's right to the throne.

Mystery Bodies

In 1674, two small bodies were found hidden beneath a staircase in the Tower. The king at the time, Charles II, believed they belonged to the princes. He had the bodies reburied in Westminster Abbey. The bones were examined in the 1930s, and found to belong to two young people of the same age as the princes, but there was no definite proof of their identity.

The two young princes were seen less and less often playing in the Tower of London—and finally disappeared.

The Pretender

In 1497, a young man named Perkin Warbeck claimed the throne of England. He said he was Prince Richard, and had been released from the Tower by the men who came to kill his brother. Warbeck attracted followers who saw the chance to gain political advantage, whether or not they believed his story. However, he was captured, tried, and executed by King Henry VII.

16

CHAPTER 3

BEYOND THE KNOWN WORLD

The Age of Exploration, from the early 1400s to the early 1600s, takes its name from the voyages made by European sailors. They made their way across the Indian Ocean to India and Southeast Asia, and across the Atlantic to America. Europeans made contact with other peoples, many for the first time.

Over the Horizon

As more people began to travel, more people disappeared. Ships sailed over the horizon—and were never seen again. Entire communities vanished without a trace. Meanwhile, Europe's cities grew and it became easier for people to disappear among the crowds in the streets.

The first False Dmitry (*see opposite*) visited King Sigismund III of Poland to get support for his claim to the Russian throne.

The Prince with Powers

One country particularly affected by mysterious disappearances was Russia. The youngest son of Russian Emperor Ivan IV, known as Ivan the Terrible, disappeared in uncertain circumstances in 1591, some years after his father had died. It was widely suspected the nine-year-old Dmitry Ivanovich had been murdered. However, in about 1600, a young man appeared in Moscow who claimed to be the missing prince. He was skilled at horse riding, and could read, which was rare at the time; he was fluent in Russian, French, and Polish. With the backing of some Polish nobles, the young man fought the Russian army to take the place of Tsar Boris Godunov.

In 1605, Godunov died suddenly. The timing was just right for Dmitry Ivanovich, who rode into Moscow to a great welcome from the people, who had never liked Boris Godunov. Even Prince Dmitry's own mother said she "recognized" him as her son—although there was never any hard evidence of his identity. Only a year later, however, Dmitry was murdered by his own nobles, who suspected that he was attacking their Russian customs.

False Princes

Dmitry became known as False Dmitry. He was followed by two more pretenders claiming the throne. In 1607, False Dmitry II even gained the support of the wife of the first False Dmitry. He raised an army and conquered southern Russia, but was killed in 1610 by a rival. False Dmitry III claimed the throne in 1611. When his forces were defeated, he was caught and secretly executed.

False Dmitry's real identity and his character and abilities have never been fully explained.

17

LOST EXPLORERS

Many explorers who set out never returned. Some probably died when their ships sank, while others may have been killed by hostile peoples or died from hunger or cold weather in new lands.

Never Heard from Again

In 1500, the King of Portugal, Manuel I, decided to join the search for new lands. He asked Gaspar Corte-Real to sail west to look for a sea route to the Spice Islands of Southeast Asia. Corte-Real and his brother Miguel sailed to Greenland, which they mistakenly thought was Asia.

The next year, they set out again with three ships. They sailed northwest until it grew so cold that the sea was frozen. The brothers headed south, and became the first Europeans to land in Labrador and Newfoundland, in Canada. Corte-Real captured 57 native men, whom he sent home with his brother to be sold as slaves. Corte-Real sailed on with one ship—and was never heard of again. The following year, Miguel Corte-Real sailed off to find his brother, but he too failed to return.

Gaspar Corte-Real has a place on Portugal's Monument to the Explorers, together with his brother, Miguel, and their father, João.

Cast Adrift

The English explorer Henry Hudson sailed three times to North America to look for a route to Asia. He discovered the Hudson River and, later, Hudson's Bay in Canada. On his final voyage, his ship became stuck in ice for months. When the ice thawed in 1611, most of Hudson's frustrated crew refused to obey his orders. They cast Hudson adrift with six others. They were never heard of again. In 1959, however, a rock was found in Ontario, Canada, carved with the letters: HH 1612 CAPTIVE. Was this a clue that somehow Hudson had managed to survive the icy water?

Unknown Fate

A similar fate happened to the Italian explorer Giovanni Caboto, known in English as John Cabot. Sailing on behalf of the British king, Cabot reached the American coast in 1497. He probably landed somewhere in Newfoundland. A year later, Cabot set off again with five ships loaded with goods to trade with native peoples in Canada. He never returned—or so people thought. In the early 2000s, a historian found evidence that one of the men who sailed with Cabot was living in London some years later. Perhaps the great seafarer had returned to England after all. If he did, however, all records of his great feat of discovery have now been lost.

Henry Hudson was cast adrift with his young son, five men, and some food and cooking equipment.

19

THE LOST COLONY

One of the oldest mysteries in American history began in 1585, when the explorer Sir Walter Raleigh sent a group of English settlers to Roanoke Island, off the coast of North Carolina. It was the first English settlement in America—but it vanished in mysterious circumstances only a few years later.

Life in Roanoke was hard. There was not enough food, and the local peoples were hostile. In 1587, the colony's governor, John White, sailed back to England to ask for government help. White's return was delayed after England went to war against Spain, and he only returned three years later, in 1590.

This image shows the baptism of Virginia Dare, the first English child to be born in America.

A Single Clue

White found the settlement deserted. The only clue about what had happened was one word carved into wood: CROATOAN. Croatoan was the name of a nearby island (now called Hatteras), so White guessed the colonists might have moved there. However, it was also the name of the hostile people who lived on the island.

White did not have the chance to find out what the sign meant. A storm prevented him visiting Croatoan Island. The next day, the ship he was sailing in left for England.

Mysterious Stories

Some people believe the colonists had moved north to live with friendly Native Americans. There were reports of white children being found living among native peoples. The descendants of local Native Americans tell old stories that their ancestors took the settlers in. Other people argue that Spanish colonists from Mexico had destroyed the colony. They wanted to prevent the English from having a presence in North America.

Tell-Tale Artifacts

In the late 1990s, archaeologists—or experts who study the remains of the past—found English artifacts some 50 miles (80 kilometers) from Roanoke Island, on Hatteras Island. One of the artifacts was a ring with the crest of the family of a man known to have been among the colonists. Perhaps there was a link between the settlers and the local people after all.

21

CHAPTER 4
EXPLANATIONS WANTED

During the 1800s, inventions such as photography made it far more difficult for people to disappear or to go unrecognized. Newspapers and "wanted" posters carried images to help identify criminals, for example. Governments also kept better records of people, noting when they were born and when they died.

Early wanted posters featured only rough sketches of culprits or no pictures at all.

A Letter L and a Shotgun

It was still possible to go missing, however. In 1848, the explorer Ludwig Leichhardt and six men set out to travel across Australia, but failed to arrive. Search parties found trees carved with the letter L, for Leichhardt, but it seemed the men had died in the Great Sandy Desert. Around 1900, an Aboriginal person discovered an old shotgun in Northwest Australia, with a name plate inscribed "Ludwig Leichhardt 1848," so experts believe the explorer made it at least two-thirds of the way across Australia before he died.

Mystery Bay

Also in Australia, in 1880, a surveyor named Lamont Young headed toward some new gold fields in New South Wales. He and his assistant hired a small boat and with three local men headed north up the coast. Next day, the boat was found washed up on the shore with a bullet in one side. It was empty apart from some rocks, the men's clothing, and Young's books and papers. There was no clue to what had happened to the men. A local spiritualist later claimed that Young's ghost had appeared and told him the men had been murdered by three strangers. The place where the men went missing is now called Mystery Bay.

This special map was published to celebrate an earlier journey by Ludwig Leichhardt.

Vanished from a Train

In 1890, in France, the cinema pioneer Louis Le Prince boarded a train in Dijon, headed to Paris. He never arrived, and neither his body nor his luggage were ever found. Some people said he had killed himself, and others claimed that he went missing in order to start a new life. Others thought his disappearance was the result of foul play. Some claimed he had been killed on the orders of the US pioneer of cinema, Thomas Edison. Seven years after Le Prince's disappearance, Edison tried to get a court to declare that he was the only inventor of cinematography, or moving pictures.

THE LOST EXPEDITION

The disappearance of the British explorer John Franklin and his crew in the Arctic in 1843 began a search to discover their fate that lasted for well over a century. Franklin was the most famous British explorer of the age, and was a national hero. Even though he was nearly 60 years old, he set out with two ships, the *Erebus* and *Terror*, which were equipped with all the most up-to-date equipment, and enough canned food for three years.

Into the North

The ships were seen heading north in summer 1845, but nothing more was heard from them. After two years, Franklin's wife Jane urged the British Admiralty to send a search party. In fact, it was another year before the Admiralty offered a reward for the discovery of any clues about the sailors' fate. The reward encouraged many ships to head to the Arctic to look for Franklin and his crew. At one time, at least 12 expeditions were involved in the search, but the men were never found alive.

Sir John Franklin's expedition ships sailed between huge icebergs in the Arctic Ocean.

Bones Tell Tales

In 1854, a Scottish explorer named John Rae visited the region. Inuit told him that the two ships had become stuck in the ice off King William Island in summer 1846. Franklin died on the island a year later—his death was recorded in a note later found on the island. Rae reported that the other men had eventually died of the cold and of starvation. Some had even eaten their dead comrades to try to stay alive. Rae's story caused a sensation. Still, examination of bones found in the late twentieth century showed that his account was correct. The bones also showed something else: it seemed that the sailors might have been poisoned by lead, either in the water pipes on board the ships or from the large cans of food they used.

In 1859, searchers discovered a cairn, or pile of stones, containing messages outlining the fate of Franklin's expedition.

THE GHOST SHIP

Some of the most remarkable disappearances of all have happened at sea—and the most famous of all was the *Mary Celeste*. The ship was an American brigantine, or cargo ship. It had formerly been known as *Amazon*, but like many ships had had its name changed. It was found abandoned by another ship, the *Dei Gratia*, near the Azores Islands in the Atlantic in December 1872.

All 10 people who had sailed on the ship were missing, but otherwise the ship was in good order. Some of its sails had been raised. The lifeboat was missing, but none of the personal belongings of the captain or crew had been taken. None of them were ever heard from again. The ship's name became a common phrase to refer to any unexplained disappearance.

This painting shows the *Mary Celeste* in 1861, when it was known as *Amazon*.

The Bermuda Triangle

Some people claim the *Mary Celeste* was a victim of the Bermuda Triangle, an area of the Atlantic Ocean off the eastern United States and the islands of the Caribbean. The area is said to experience many mysterious disappearances of ships and airplanes. Some people say this is because it has many sudden tropical storms, called cyclones. Others have reported strange events in the region, such as ships' compasses not working, which may be the result of supernatural forces at work.

Attacked by a Sea Monster?

At a hearing into the mystery, people put forward ideas about what might have happened. One was that the crew had mutinied, or turned against the captain; however, that did not explain what had become of the crew. Another idea was that the crew had been killed by the crew of the *Dei Gratia*. They would have been entitled to claim the abandoned ship and its cargo for themselves.

This illustration imagines an alien spacecraft following a fighter plane during World War II (1939–1945). Aliens are sometimes blamed for disappearances in the Bermuda Triangle.

When the hearing could not decide on the crew's fate, people began to put forward other explanations. They included a story that the ship's crew had been killed by a giant squid, or that the crew had been knocked overboard by a spinning column of water, called a waterspout. Some people claimed that the crew had been taken by aliens or by magical forces.

THE EMPTY LIGHTHOUSE

The island of Eilean Mor is not much more than a rock in the Outer Hebrides, a group of islands off the west coast of Scotland. In recent history no one has lived there, apart from the keepers of its lighthouse. In 1900, however, when a boat carried a replacement keeper to the island, he found it mysteriously deserted.

Haunted by Spirits

Local people said Eilean Mor was haunted by spirits, and refused to stay there overnight. Joseph Moore, the replacement keeper, felt a sense of doom as he climbed up the steps cut into the cliff. None of the three keepers had come to meet him when he fired a flare, or signal rocket.

Nobody knows why the lighthouse keepers would feel frightened inside a solid stone and concrete lighthouse.

At the lighthouse, Moore found the door unlocked. Inside the kitchen, he found uneaten food and a chair that had fallen over, as if someone had suddenly jumped up. The clock had stopped. A single coat hung in the hall, which suggested that one of the keepers had rushed outside without it, even though it was a bitterly cold winter. Moore could only think the men had been blown over a cliff in a storm.

A Strange Storm

Other investigators soon arrived to try to find out what had happened to the missing men. They looked for clues in the lighthouse logbook. The final entry had been made 10 days before Moore had arrived. The log recorded a storm so strong that it reduced the men to crying as they prayed for it to end, even though they were inside a new lighthouse.

The men seemed to feel that this was not a normal storm. The last entry in the log said the storm had finished and ended with the odd phrase, "God is over all." No one knew what that might mean—and, in fact, no storm had even been visible from nearby islands at all on the dates recorded in the logbook.

An Unexplained Moaning

The investigators concluded that the three men must have been knocked into the sea by a wave when they were trying to secure a storage crate on the landing platform at the bottom of the cliff. However, that did not explain why no bodies were ever washed ashore, nor the strange moaning other keepers reported hearing when the wind blew at night over the following decades.

29

CHAPTER 5

LOST CONTACT

From the early 1900s, technology made it harder for people to disappear. In 1910, Hawley Harvey Crippen fled from London to the United States after murdering his wife. The captain of his ship recognized Crippen and sent a telegram to the London police, who had a policeman meet Crippen's ship and arrest him. Crippen was returned to London, tried, and executed. Nevertheless, there were still some very disturbing disappearances.

The Wild Bunch are said to be the most successful gang of train robbers in history.

The Fate of the Outlaws

One story that fascinated the public was the fate of the American outlaws Butch Cassidy and the Sundance Kid. The pair were the leaders of a gang called the Wild Bunch, which had robbed trains and banks around Utah. Wanting to give up crime, the outlaws headed to South America, where they worked as miners in Bolivia.

However, the pair are believed to have gone back to their old ways and carried out a robbery in 1908. The Bolivian army hunted them down and surrounded them in a wooden shack. The Bolivians announced that the outlaws died in a shootout with their pursuers. But did they? No one ever identified the bodies—and there were a number of rumors in the 1920s that Butch Cassidy at least had survived. He was reported to have been seen in Wyoming and Utah by old friends and by members of his family who claimed to have recognized him.

Butch Cassidy and the Sundance Kid bought a wooden ranch cabin in Argentina, where they lived for just a few months in 1901.

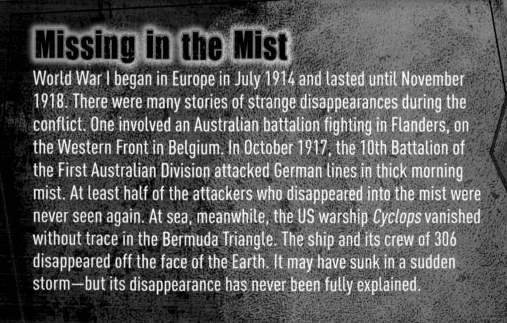

Missing in the Mist

World War I began in Europe in July 1914 and lasted until November 1918. There were many stories of strange disappearances during the conflict. One involved an Australian battalion fighting in Flanders, on the Western Front in Belgium. In October 1917, the 10th Battalion of the First Australian Division attacked German lines in thick morning mist. At least half of the attackers who disappeared into the mist were never seen again. At sea, meanwhile, the US warship *Cyclops* vanished without trace in the Bermuda Triangle. The ship and its crew of 306 disappeared off the face of the Earth. It may have sunk in a sudden storm—but its disappearance has never been fully explained.

During World War I, soldiers from Britain, Australia, and New Zealand landed at Gallipoli, at the point where the Mediterranean Sea is joined by a narrow channel to the Black Sea. They wanted to attack Turkey, which was fighting on the other side in the war, together with Germany and Austria. The Allied troops were trapped along the sea, trying to fight their way inland.

Disappearing in the Forest

Among the Allied troops was a battalion of the 5th Norfolk Regiment. It was made up of about 220 men recruited from the workers on the English king's country estate at Sandringham in Norfolk. The men were sick and tired after the long voyage from Great Britain, and when they went into action, they soon became separated from the main attacking force. Still, the Norfolks charged into a forest to try to capture a heavily defended ridge—and were never heard from again.

The British assumed they had been captured by the Turks, but the Turks denied any knowledge of the men. After the end of the war, however, Allied researchers found bodies near a farmhouse in the woods. The badges on their uniforms suggested they were the Norfolks. It seemed they had died bravely in battle.

Allied troops came ashore at Gallipoli in February 1915.

The Missing Writer

The US writer Ambrose Bierce was famous for writing ghost stories—but nothing he wrote was as strange as his own disappearance. In 1913, aged 71, Bierce headed to Mexico, where the Mexican Revolution was going on. He wrote to a friend: "I leave here tomorrow for an unknown destination." No one ever heard from him again. There were reports that he was killed, but no evidence suggested he had even left the United States.

Extraterrestrial Kidnap

A new twist to the story came on the 50th anniversary of the battalion's disappearance in 1965. A New Zealand witness said that he and his coworkers had watched five or six strangely shaped clouds that hung above the battlefield that day. They were long and thin, like cigars, and hung very still, even though it was a windy day. One of the clouds floated down to the ground, and the Norfolks marched into it. It rose into the air and moved away with the other clouds, taking the Norfolks with it. The next year, another witness backed up the story.

Ambrose Bierce went to Mexico to visit with the rebel leader Pancho Villa, and never came home.

The 1960s was a period when the first humans visited space. People were growing more interested in space travel. The idea that aliens had taken the soldiers soon spread. It became so popular that many people believed the British army was deliberately covering up the true story, because it would have proven beyond doubt that alien life existed.

33

AMELIA EARHART

In the 1920s, the US pilot Amelia Earhart became one of the most famous people in the world. In 1932, she became the first woman to fly across the Atlantic, and broke many other flying records at the same time. In 1937, she set out to become the first person to fly around the whole world. It was her final trip.

Going Silent

Earhart and her navigator, Fred Noonan, planned to travel in a series of steps in her famous Lockheed L10 Electra. They flew from Miami to South America, then to Africa and India, before setting out across the vast Pacific Ocean. They reached New Guinea in late June 1937, having already flown 22,000 miles (35,000 km).

The plane took off from New Guinea and flew toward Howland Island, about 2,500 miles (4,020 km) away. On the way, the airplane lost radio contact with people on the ground. What happened to the two aviators remains unknown.

Amelia Earhart had only 7,000 miles (11,000 km) of her around-the-world trip left when she vanished in the Pacific Ocean.

Looking for Answers

The most likely explanation is that they crashed into the sea and died, or landed on a remote island where they survived until they starved to death. Some people said Noonan was a drinker who had become lost over the Pacific. There were even claims that Earhart had been captured by the Japanese, because this was a time of growing tension between Japan and the United States in the years before World War II (1939–1945). One story said that she was an American spy working for President Franklin D. Roosevelt.

Some people believe Earhart landed on Gardner Island, or Nikumaroro, but there is no definite proof of this.

A Lasting Mystery

Despite extensive searches of islands where the pair could have landed, no definite proof of their fate was ever found. In the 1940s, Earhart was even reported to have been found living under a new name in New Jersey. The mystery continues to fascinate people. The search for evidence goes on. A number of pieces of wreckage have been located in different places. Researchers are still studying human bones found in 1940 on Gardner Island, south of Howland Island. Could this have been the final destination for the most famous female pilot in the world?

THE MISSING VILLAGE

On a freezing night in December 1930, a fur trapper named Joe Labelle walked into the remote Inuit village of Anjikuni in Kivalliq, Nunavut, in Canada. Labelle had visited the village before and was seeking a warm place to rest. When he arrived, however, he noticed that the streets were oddly quiet.

Looking into the huts, he realized that the 30 or so inhabitants had all disappeared. There were no fires lit, but everyone's possessions had been left in perfect order. Wherever the villagers had gone, they had not taken their rifles or coats, or even supplies of food. Just outside the village, Labelle said he found a fire that was still burning. There was no one around it, however, and a pot of stew on top of it had become burned and blackened.

Inuit in northern Canada lived mainly in villages of wooden huts. When traveling, they built ice shelters called igloos.

Graves Without Bodies

Labelle had heard Inuit stories of spirits who lived in the woods, and he became spooked. When he calmed down, he went to a telegraph office and sent a message to the Royal Canadian Mounted Police (RCMP), or Mounties. As the Mounties traveled to Anjikuni, they passed a home where the residents reported seeing a huge light flying toward the village. The Mounties themselves saw blue lights over Anjikuni.

At Anjikuni, the Mounties confirmed that the village was deserted. Not only that. At the edge of the settlement, they found bodies had been dug up from the graveyard— even though the frozen ground was as hard as rock. The Mounties also found husky dogs that had starved to death. Despite Labelle having discovered a fire still burning, the RCMP decided the village had been abandoned for at least two months.

According to official records, the RCMP never investigated an incident at Anjikuni.

Cover-Up or Hoax?

This was the story published in a book called *Stranger than Science* in 1959 by US author Frank Edwards. However, the RCMP said that the event had never happened. Later, researchers began to suspect that Labelle had made the story up—or that, more likely, the whole incident had simply been imagined by Frank Edwards.

CHAPTER 6

THE HUNT GOES ON

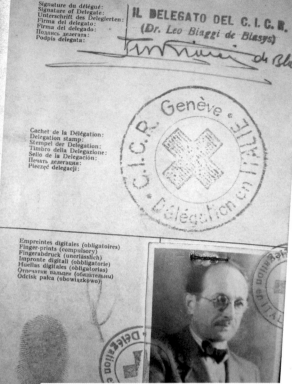

Even since the middle of the twentieth century, when it might seem impossible for someone to disappear, mysteries still remained. Some concerned the fate of the Nazis, who governed Germany in the 1930s and during World War II.

This is the false passport the Nazi Adolf Eichmann used to escape from Germany to Argentina.

Nazi Hunters

At the end of the conflict, after Germany was defeated, many senior Nazis simply disappeared. It was thought they were smuggled to safety by their supporters. Some were said to have escaped to South America, where the Nazis had political admirers.

In 1960, Israeli agents seized Ricardo Klement, who worked in a car factory in Buenos Aires, Argentina. Klement turned out to be Adolf Eichmann, a senior Nazi who was wanted for his part in the Holocaust, or the murder of millions of Jews and other people. Eichmann was tried, found guilty, and executed. Other Nazis are believed to have successfully avoided capture. However, former Nazi officials were still being found by so-called Nazi hunters and and put on trial as late as 2018.

Hiding in the Hotel

A notorious disappearance in the 1960s was that of the former Hollywood producer and aviation pioneer Howard Hughes. One of the world's most famous men, Hughes became a recluse, which means he never went outside or met other people. He became obsessed with avoiding other people's germs. For a decade from about 1966 to 1976, he lived only in hotels around the world, but mostly in Las Vegas. At first, he hired the entire top penthouse floor of the hotel. Then bought the whole hotel! In one story, he also bought the next-door hotel—just so that he could switch off the flashing lights it used at night.

As a young man, Howard Hughes set many flying records and was involved in aircraft development.

Fight Over the Will

Hughes' secretive life led to many stories about him after his death in 1976. A number of people claimed that they had secretly met Hughes, who had promised them a share of his fortune. A gas-station owner in Nevada claimed to have found Hughes lying alongside the highway. In what was said to be Hughes' will, the gas-station owner received $156 million—but the will was soon ruled to be a fake.

THE MISSING HIJACKER

Just before Thanksgiving in 1971, a passenger threatened to set off a bomb on a flight from Portland to Seattle. He asked for $200,000 to be ready for him at Seattle, together with four parachutes. In Seattle, the man let everyone go except the pilots. He told them to fly to Mexico and shut them in the cockpit. About 20 minutes later, an indicator showed that the plane's rear door had been opened. The hijacker had jumped out with the ransom money.

The hijacked Boeing 727, similar to this one, flew too high to make it easy for anyone to jump out safely using a parachute.

Jumping into Nowhere

The hijacking began a mystery that has lasted nearly 50 years. The hijacker had bought his ticket in the name Dan Cooper, although he is usually referred to as D. B. Cooper. He was a middle-aged man in a business suit. No one has ever identified him.

Police retraced the airplane's route to try to figure out where the hijacker jumped off. They decided it was near Mount Saint Helens, in Washington State. Despite searches on the ground and from the air, nothing was discovered. It seemed the man had escaped —or had jumped to his death. It was unlikely anyone could survive a parachute jump from an airplane at high altitude.

Follow the Money

The Federal Bureau of Investigation (FBI) circulated the serial numbers of the bills included in the ransom money, but none of them was ever spent. Seven years later, a hunter in Washington State found the remains of a printed instruction card about how to open the rear door of an airplane like the one in the hijack. In 1980, a young boy playing in a stream near Vancouver found three packets of decayed cash still held together by rubber bands. The FBI confirmed that they came from the ransom money. No other banknotes from the ransom money were ever found.

Escape from Alcatraz

In 1962, three inmates escaped from Alcatraz, a prison on an island in San Francisco Bay. Frank Morris and brothers John and Clarence Anglin dug a tunnel through air vents. One night, they left dummies in their beds and crept down to the shore. They used an inflatable raft to sail into the bay. No trace of them was ever found, and the FBI reported they had drowned in the cold water. However, in the 2010s, people began to claim that they had survived. The Anglin family even claimed to have a photograph showing John and Clarence later in their lives. However, there is no definite proof of the men's fates.

41

THE MISSING AIRLINER

On March 8, 2014, Malaysia Airlines Flight 370 took off from Kuala Lumpur in Malaysia, heading for Beijing. Soon afterward, it vanished from radar screens over the South China Sea. No trace of the airplane or the 239 people on board has been found, despite the most expensive search effort in aviation history.

Last Contact

After the airliner's last communication, military radar continued to track it for over an hour. It showed that the aircraft had left its planned course, although no one knows why. The first search efforts targeted the South China and Andaman Seas, but then Australia released data from one of its satellites that suggested the aircraft had likely crashed in the southern Indian Ocean. In 2015 and 2016, a few pieces of debris washed up around the shores of the ocean that came from MH370. Aircraft carry beacons that are meant to give out signals if they crash into water, but no signals were ever located. A three-year search found no definite clues as to what had happened to the airplane.

The Malaysian Airlines Boeing 777, which looked like this aircraft, stopped making radio contact 38 minutes after takeoff.

Sudden Distress

One explanation for the disappearance was that there had been a sudden disaster that left the pilots unable to send a distress message before the airplane crashed into the sea. Another was that one of the pilots had deliberately crashed the aircraft. In another story, hijackers seized the aircraft and caused it to crash. None of these explanations has been verified.

US Navy ships joined the search for MH370. They used sensors to try to locate the aircraft's beacons.

Death in the Consulate

In October 2018, a Saudi journalist named Jamal Khashoggi entered the Saudi consulate in Istanbul, Turkey. He never left. The Turks said he was killed by a hit squad who had flown in from Saudi Arabia. The Saudis said he had been killed by agents acting without orders. Many people believed Khashoggi had been targeted for criticizing the Saudi government.

Still Missing

One story was that the plane's passengers and crew were living on an island or had been taken prisoner somewhere. The disaster is one of the great unexplained disappearances of the modern age. Although technology can track almost any location on the planet, it seems that it is still as possible for people to vanish without trace as it was thousands of years ago.

43

TIMELINE

878 — The Twelfth Imam, Muhammad al-Mahdi, disappears; his followers believe he remains hidden on Earth.

1412 — Welsh rebel leader Owain Glyndwr disappears. Some claim he will return to help the Welsh in their greatest need.

1483 — The young Edward V and his brother disappear from the Tower of London.

1498 — Explorer John Cabot and his crew fail to return from a voyage to North America, although one of his crew is reportedly living in London many years later.

1501 — The explorer Gaspar Corte-Real vanishes. His brother later vanishes without a trace while searching for him.

1578 — King Sebastian of Portugal disappears. Some believe he will one day return.

1590 — The English colony at Roanoke Island is discovered abandoned after three years.

1600 — "False Dmitry" claims to be Dmitry Ivanovich, heir to the Russian throne. He has unexplained abilities.

1611 — Henry Hudson and six companions are cast adrift. Apart from a strange rock carving, they are never heard from again.

1843 British explorer Sir John Franklin and his expedition go missing in the Arctic. They inspire many search missions.

1872 The *Mary Celeste* is found floating abandoned in the Atlantic Ocean.

1890 French cinema pioneer Louis Le Prince boards a train in Paris and is never seen or heard from again.

1900 Three lighthouse keepers vanish from the island of Eilean Mor, leaving a diary entry saying, "God is over all."

1915 A unit of Britain's Norfolk Regiment vanishes from the battlefield at Gallipoli in Turkey.

1930 A fur trapper reports the disappearance of an entire Inuit village in northern Canada after mysterious lights are seen in the sky.

1937 Aviator Amelia Earhart and her navigator, Fred Noonan, go missing over the Pacific Ocean on a global flight.

1971 Hijacker "Dan Cooper" vanishes after parachuting from an airliner.

2014 Flight MH370 vanishes. The fate of the 239 people on board remains unknown.

2018 Journalist Jamal Khashoggi is murdered in the Saudi consulate in Turkey. His body is not found.

GLOSSARY

aliens Beings from other planets.

altitude The height of something above the ground.

artifacts Objects made by people.

aviators People who fly aircraft.

battalion An infantry unit in an army.

beacons Devices that give out signals using light or sound.

civilization A highly advanced society.

colony A settlement founded in another country.

conquest Taking control of a place by military force.

coronation A ceremony to crown a king or queen.

debate A formal discussion of different views about a subject.

deputies Assistants.

descendants People who descended from a particular ancestor.

doom Death or destruction.

executed Killed as a legal punishment.

fate What will happen to someone, particularly with regard to his or her death.

fluent Able to speak a language easily.

heir A person who inherits a title or belongings when someone dies.

hijacker Someone who seizes a vehicle or airplane and makes it go to a particular destination.

hit squad A team of killers.

horizon The line where the land or ocean seems to meet the sky.

husky dogs A type of dog used in snowy places to pull sleds.

identity Who or what a person is.

imposters People who pretend to be someone else to deceive people.

Inuit A traditional people who live in America, Europe, and Asia within the Arctic Circle.

lead A soft metal that can be poisonous to people.

log An official daily written record.

merchants People who trade goods over long distances.

navigator Someone who plots the course of a journey or voyage.

occultation The state of being hidden from view.

pardon A document freeing someone of punishment for a crime.

penthouse A luxury accommodation on the top floor of a building.

pioneer One of the first people to do something.

portraits Drawings or paintings of people's faces.

pretenders People who falsely claim a title or position.

radar A device that uses radio waves to locate objects.

ransom A sum of money paid to stop something bad from happening.

remote Isolated.

satellites Space objects moving around Earth that are used for communications

telegram A message sent by radio telegraph.

will A document that says what someone wants to happen to their possessions after they die.

46

FOR FURTHER READING

BOOKS

Lassieur, Allison. *Unsolved Historical Mysteries* (Unsolved Mystery Files). North Mankato, MN: Capstone Press, 2015.

Loh-Hagen, Virginia. *Mysterious Vanishings* (Stranger Than Fiction). Ann Arbor, MI: Cherry Lake Publishing, 2018.

Mysteries of the Unknown: Inside the World of the Strange and Unexplained. New York, NY: Time-Life Books, 2015.

Stine, Megan. *Where Is the Bermuda Triangle?* (Where Is?). New York, NY: Penguin Group, 2018.

WEBSITES

9 Mysterious Disappearances of People Other Than Amelia Earhart—https://www.britannica.com/list/9-mysterious-disappearances-of-people-other-than-amelia-earhart
More information about more mysteriously missing people.

D. B. Cooper—*http://nymag.com/news/features/39593*
The story of the 1971 hijacking in Washington State and the possible identity of the hijacker.

MH370—*http://edition.cnn.com/2018/05/29/asia/mh370-search-ends-intl/index.html*
Details about the search for the missing flight MH370.

Unsolved Disappearances—*www.livescience.com/55591-unsolved-deaths-and-disappearances.html*
Some of the most mysterious disappearances in history.

INDEX